Neighbourhood
Watch

Alan Ayckbourn

A SAMUEL FRENCH ACTING EDITION

SAMUEL
FRENCH

FOUNDED 1830

SAMUELFRENCH.COM
SAMUELFRENCH-LONDON.CO.UK

FOR PRODUCTION ENQUIRIES

Plays@SamuelFrench-London.co.uk
020-7255-4302/01

Each title is subject to availability from Samuel French, depending upon country of performance. Please be aware that *NEIGHBOURHOOD WATCH* may not be licensed by Samuel French in your territory. Professional and amateur producers should contact the nearest Samuel French office or licensing partner to verify availability.

The professional rights in this play are controlled by Casarotto Ramsay and Associates, Waverley House, 7-12 Noel Street, London, W1F 8GQ.

MUSIC USE NOTE

Licensees are solely responsible for obtaining formal written permission from copyright owners to use copyrighted music in the performance of this play and are strongly cautioned to do so. If no such permission is obtained by the licensee, then the licensee must use only original music that the licensee owns and controls. Licensees are solely responsible and liable for all music clearances and shall indemnify the copyright owners of the play(s) and their licensing agent, Samuel French, against any costs, expenses, losses and liabilities arising from the use of music by licensees. Please contact the appropriate music licensing authority in your territory for the rights to any incidental music.

IMPORTANT BILLING AND CREDIT REQUIREMENTS

If you have obtained performance rights to this title, please refer to your licensing agreement for important billing and credit requirements.

NEIGHBOURHOOD WATCH was first produced at the Stephen Joseph Theatre, Scarborough on 8th September 2011. The performance was directed by Alan Ayckbourn, designed by Pip Leckenby, with lighting designed by Mick Hughes. The cast was as follows:

DOROTHY	Eileen Battye
ROD	Terence Booth
LUTHER	Phil Cheadle
MARTIN	Matthew Cottle
GARETH	Richard Derrington
AMY	Frances Grey
MAGDA	Amy Loughton
HILDA	Alexandra Mathie

CHARACTERS

MARTIN MASSIE, 40s
HILDA MASSIE, his sister, a little older
LUTHER BRADLEY, 30s
MAGDA BRADLEY, his wife, 20s
GARETH JANNER, 40s
AMY JANNER, his wife, 30s
ROD TRUSSER, 60s
DOROTHY DOGGETT, 60s

SETTING

Martin and Hilda's sitting room at number three,
the Bluebell Hill Development

TIME

Now and four months ago.

PROLOGUE

(Today.)

*(**HILDA** appears in a single spot. She is addressing us all plus a few more who are unseen, including several dozen of the world's press. Being an unassuming, fairly ordinary 50-year-old woman quite unused to this sort of thing, she is understandably nervous initially but as she speaks she gains in confidence. There is the occasional flicker of a flash bulb. To start with she consults her notes.)*

HILDA. Dear friends. It is my pleasure to officially open the Martin Massie Memorial Park.

Three months ago, I said farewell, in this world at least, to my dear brother, Martin. We'd been extremely close all our lives. Indeed my first memory, as his older sister, was looking after Martin. Our dear mother, after giving birth to him, was in frail health for her all too brief remaining days.

As a sister only a handful of years older than he, I soon grew used to the routine day to day caring of my little brother, the nurturing, the caring, the cleaning – all the tasks usually coped with by a mother.

But as the years went by, as we both grew older, as my responsibilities grew less onerous and as my brother became increasingly self-sufficient, very soon our roles became in many ways reversed. Martin developed into a strong-minded, independent, able-bodied young man and began gradually to take care of me, his sister – *(smiling)* – who was no less able-bodied I hasten to add, but nonetheless a young woman with the natural

1

limitations of physical strength and the vulnerabilities of her gender.

And so, as time passed, his older sister began to rely on him. Initially, as I say, on his role as physical protector but then, gradually, on his wisdom and judgement as well. I soon grew to realise that my brother was, from an early age, already someone quite remarkable.

From our formative years at the insistence of our firm and at times strict father (these days indeed he would be regarded as over-strict), Martin and I had both become devout Christians.

But, as many of us who attempt to adhere to that creed are only too aware, adherence to the Christian faith requires very much more than lip service. It is above all a faith that demands that, when asked of you, those spiritual beliefs are translated into active deeds. How many of us fail that test?

But my brother never waivered. Whenever the call came for action, no matter how daunting or dangerous the odds, Martin was there to respond. To respond as my brother, to respond as a man and above all to respond as a Christian.

Is it not typical of him that he died protecting his loved ones, protecting his home, unarmed and unafraid, clasping in his hand the symbol of his belief, the final words on his lips the name of our Blessed Saviour?

Martin was a man driven by faith and powered by love. Love for his fellow men and women. *(Faltering)* I am privileged and humbly grateful to have been a recipient of a small part of that greater love.

(Recovering) Why did Martin need to die so tragically and prematurely? What was in God's purpose? Over the weeks I have prayed for the answer.

I believe it to be this. With the founding of The Bluebell Hill Development Neighbourhood Watch

Scheme, Martin laid down his blueprint, his dream, his plan for a better world.

True that dream has faltered; beset by human, temporary frailties, it has suffered set-backs. But, dear friends, it must never be allowed to die. We, the currently insignificant few, must go forth and multiply. Increase our number until the insignificant few grow into the significant multitude. It must be allowed to grow until every parent loves the child; every child respects the parent. Every husband honours the wife; every wife respects the husband. Till every neighbour reaches in friendship to neighbour. Till no stranger is turned away from our door. Till love becomes the only arbiter, and God the final authority. Let us then carry the fight forward as Martin would have wanted. As long as I have breath in my body I am ready to help reignite his glorious flame that has been left to flicker and grow dim.

It is my joy today not only to open the Martin Massie Memorial Park – many a time he delighted in looking out over this field – but also to unveil his memorial. Why this particular image, I hear you asking? Well, I have chosen a symbol which, though reflecting England and all things English, also reaches out in non-denominational greeting to every corner of the world, to all mankind. It's an image that was also personally dear to Martin. He believed it stood for the important things – all sadly unfashionable these days. Important things like Respectability and Decency, Honour and Moral Strength, Courage and Spiritual Conviction. It is with pride and pleasure that I declare this park open. Thank you.

(The band strikes up. The light fades on **HILDA**. *As the music continues, the lights come on:)*

Act I

Scene One

(Four months earlier.)

*(**MARTIN** and **HILDA***'s sitting room in their house at
number three The Bluebell Hill Development.)*

*(The setting is representational and by no means
realistic. References to objects, patio and internal doors,
walls, etc. are invisible.)*

*(We are largely asked to imagine, therefore, the large
living room of a detached modern home, with a picture
window along one wall with sliding patio doors opening
on to an (also unseen) large-ish back garden. Two other
doors, on the other side of the space, lead off, one to the
hall, the front door and the rest of the house; the other
door via a passage to the kitchen. These two entrances
are linked via an offstage dining room.)*

*(The only visible furnishings are a trio of low, modern,
dark, neutral-coloured, slightly curved three-seater sofas
arranged in the form of an interrupted horseshoe,
the open end of which looks out on to the garden. The
sofas are adorned by several brightly-coloured pairs of
scatter cushions. Low tables service this seating area.
An additional upright chair and possibly a side table
furnish the room's perimeter. Plain and uncluttered best
describes it.)*

*(It is afternoon in early summer around tea-time and
at present **MARTIN**, in his forties, is standing at the
window admiring the garden with satisfaction.)*

MARTIN. *(looking out to the garden, calling)* You've certainly made a start out there. Well done.

HILDA. *(off)* It's a start, anyway.

MARTIN. *(calling)* I see Monty's already in pride of place. He likes it here.

HILDA. *(off)* He would.

MARTIN. *(calling)* He prefers it to number thirty-one. He would. He only had the yard before. Now he's got a whole lawn. Look at him. Mr Montmorency, master of all he surveys. All he needs now is a pond. Next thing is to dig him a pond.

HILDA. *(off)* There's enough to do on the house before we start digging ponds.

MARTIN. *(calling)* I'll dig him one, don't worry. Soon as we're straight, I'll get digging. *(Scanning the garden)* What have you done with Jesus? I can't see him anywhere.

*(**HILDA** enters with a couple of plates of nibbles. They are expecting company.)*

HILDA. *(as she enters)* Oh, he's out there.

MARTIN. Ah, yes, there he is, I see him. In the shrubbery, there, peeping out of the shrubbery. What's he doing in the bushes?

HILDA. Keeping an eye on things.

MARTIN. He's Jesus. He shouldn't be lurking in the bushes, should he?

HILDA. He's a bit – cautious, at the moment.

MARTIN. Cautious?

HILDA. He's missing his alcove. He'll be out in a day or two, you'll see. Don't rush him. He can bless things just as easily from the bushes.

*(**MARTIN** smiles and shakes his head at the turn the conversation is taking.)*

MARTIN. *(laughing)* If people could see us now they'd think we were mad, wouldn't they?

HILDA. What do you mean? We are mad. *(She laughs)* We're both completely mad, didn't you know that?

MARTIN. *(laughing)* No need to advertise it, though, is there?

HILDA. People next door'll think there's a couple of lunatics moved in.

(Standing beside him and looking out.)

Oh, look at that view. I'll never tire of that view, you know, Martin. Looking out over the field. Could be in the country, couldn't we?

MARTIN. We could be. Easily. Except for the estate. That housing estate at the bottom there.

HILDA. That's miles away.

MARTIN. Quarter of a mile, I reckon.

HILDA. Doesn't bother me.

MARTIN. All that red brick, though. Spoils the vista.

HILDA. I don't mind it. I'm glad we don't have a great high fence, not like they've got on either side. They can't have any view at all, not with those fences, surely? Can't think why they put them up, can you?

MARTIN. Security, probably. With that sort of estate down there at the bottom, you never know. People get nervous. Feel vulnerable. You can't blame them, these days.

HILDA. The woman who sold us this, old Mrs Beadie, she didn't seem to need a fence. And she was on her own in her eighties. She had more reason than most to be fearful. It didn't bother her, did it?

MARTIN. Probably couldn't afford a fence, poor soul. Single pensioners like her on fixed incomes can't splash out on fences.

HILDA. You're not planning on putting one up, are you?

MARTIN. No … I can cope. Any trouble …

HILDA. *(laughing, teasing)* Oh, yes? You and who else?

MARTIN. Me and Jesus. We'll sort them out between us, don't worry. You know, I bet all that, as far as we can see, all of it was designated green belt at one time, wasn't it? Originally? But governments, despite all their promises, they keep eating away at it. Same everywhere. Tragic. Not a blade of grass left eventually. England's green and pleasant land, all sold off. Concreted over. All in the name of progress. Personal profit.

HILDA. So long as we don't get a fence, that's all. I must get on, they'll be arriving soon.

MARTIN. How many are we expecting?

HILDA. Oh, everyone. Everybody in Bluebell Hill. The ones I didn't get to speak to, I popped cards through their door.

MARTIN. There'll be at least a hundred then, if they all come.

HILDA. They won't all come

MARTIN. You never know. Free cup of tea. They'll be beating a path.

HILDA. They won't all come …

MARTIN. Be interested to see what we've done with the place, too. I would.

HILDA. It was quite short notice. I said tea from five onwards. Some of them will probably be busy. Might be working late, you never know. Still, it's a gesture. House warming. It's a gesture, isn't it? Breaking the ice, that's all it is. I've been so busy I've hardly spoken to anyone, have you? Apart from the young woman next door. She seemed friendly. Little bit shy … I think she might be artistic. I got that impression, anyway.

MARTIN. Oh dear, oh dear, not an artist! There goes the neighbourhood. *(He laughs)* I did pass the time of day with the bloke three doors down, yesterday. Retired security bloke. Pleasant enough. Seemed a bit lonely.

HILDA. That can be your job then, cheer him up.

MARTIN. I think that might be beyond even me, from the look of him.

HILDA. I'll pop the kettle on. I've laid it all out in the dining room. Then we can invite them to wander at will. Rather than doing official conducted tours.

MARTIN. Hope they don't drop crumbs everywhere.

HILDA. They won't.

MARTIN. Spill tea all over the new carpets.

HILDA. They're not those sort of people.

MARTIN. You never know with artists. Throw tea everywhere, given half a chance.

HILDA. *(giggles)* Oh, you … If the bell goes can you let them in, I'll be in the kitchen …

MARTIN. Right. Will do.

HILDA. *(straightening a plate as she goes)* I'll leave these here, then they can top up as they pass … We can leave those garden doors open, can't we? Still quite mild.

MARTIN. Oh, yes. You never know, some of them may want to wander outside if it gets overcrowded in here.

(**HILDA** *goes out.* **MARTIN** *surveys the room.*)

(Half to himself, contentedly) Yes … yes … *(Calling)* I think you chose rightly with this wallpaper, you know, Hilda.

HILDA. *(off)* Oh. Coming round to it at last, are you? About time, too!

MARTIN. *(calling)* Yes, I should have trusted you in the first place. I ought to know better by now in matters of interior decoration, always be ruled by you. You're the artistic one. *(Turning back to the window, as he speaks)* You were right. This green, specially the paintwork, reflects the garden there, like you said … *(He breaks off as he sees something happening outside)* What the – ? What's that kid doing? What's he doing? *(Yelling out of the window)* Oy! You!

HILDA. *(off)* What's that?

MARTIN. *(calling out of the window)* What do you think you're doing? Get down off there at once! This is private property! Do you hear me?

(HILDA, alarmed by the disturbance, hurries in from the kitchen.)

HILDA. *(as she enters)* What's going on? What's the trouble?

MARTIN. *(ignoring her, yelling)* Get down off there! Get down this minute! It's some kid there, do you see?

HILDA. What's he doing? *(Calling)* Get down! Shoo! Shoo! Go away!

MARTIN. *(going out into the garden)* What's he got in his hand there …? What have you got there?

(As MARTIN goes out, HILDA hovers in the garden doorway, agitatedly.)

Careful, Martin! Do be careful. He may be armed, you never know.

(The doorbell.)

(Torn) Oh, the doorbell. *(Calling)* Be careful, Martin, careful!

MARTIN. *(off, from the garden)* Give me that! Give that to me! OW!!! You little …

HILDA. You alright?

(The doorbell rings again.)

(Flustered) Oh! Oh! Oh! I have to answer the door, Martin. I'll be back, love! Oh!

(HILDA hurries off to the front door. MARTIN returns from the garden, limping. He carries a battered clarinet case, though this is not immediately apparent.)

MARTIN. *(calling back as he goes)* Yes, you run home! Off you go! I'll know you again, young man! I'll know you! Little devil.

(He stands at the window watching the boy as presumably he runs off across the field.)

(ROD TRUSSER enters, the first of the guests. He is well built, in his sixties, a man who has evidently led an active life and is still in fair condition for his age. He strides into the room in response to the emergency.)

(**HILDA** *follows with the second of their guests,*
DOROTHY DOGGETT, *a widow also in her sixties.*)

ROD. *(as they enter)* Spot of trouble, is there?

HILDA. You alright, Martin?

MARTIN. Yes, he's … he ran away …

ROD. *(moving to the window)* Which way'd he go?

MARTIN. Across the field there towards the estate.

ROD. *(disgustedly)* Ah! Might have known it. One of them.
Where'd he come from, did you see which way?

MARTIN. *(rubbing his shin)* He was climbing over the
dividing wall to next door, there. That way. I caught
him red handed, sitting astride it.

ROD. Next door?

MARTIN. That way. From number five, is it?

DOROTHY. Oh, them.

(**ROD** *steps out into the garden, momentarily.* **MARTIN**
flexes his injured leg.)

HILDA. *(concerned)* You alright, Martin?

MARTIN. Yes, he … When I grabbed hold of him he –
kicked me, that's all. In the shin.

HILDA. Oh, dear. *(Moving to him)* Let me see.

DOROTHY. Lucky he only kicked you. He could just as soon
have knifed you, easily.

HILDA. Oh, don't say that. Do sit down, Dorothy, won't you?

DOROTHY. They all carry knives these days. Bristling with
them.

HILDA. Oh, Martin, this is Dorothy, by the way –

MARTIN. How do you do?

DOROTHY. Hallo.

HILDA. *(examining* **MARTIN**'s *leg)* – no, it looks alright, you'll
have a bit of a bruise in the morning but … Dorothy?
I'm sorry, I didn't catch your second name, Mrs –

DOROTHY. Just call me Dorothy. Everybody calls me Dorothy round here. Dorothy from number four opposite.

HILDA. This is my brother, Martin. I'm Hilda. *(To* **MARTIN***)* Please call me Hilda. Do you want something on it, Martin? Arnica?

MARTIN. No, no, it's alright.

DOROTHY. Arnica's wonderful.

HILDA. Oh yes, I swear by it.

MARTIN. *(moving to the window, evading further attention)* I'm fine, really. It's fine. *(Calling out to* **ROD***)* Any sign of him?

ROD. *(off)* No. He's gone. Little bugger's scarpered.

HILDA. *(noticing the music case)* What's this?

MARTIN. *(turning)* Eh?

HILDA. This, here? Where'd it come from?

MARTIN. That's what the kid was carrying.

HILDA. *(reaching to examine it)* Oh, what is it?

DOROTHY. Careful! Could be a gun.

HILDA. *(drawing back)* Oh!

DOROTHY. They all carry guns ...

*(***ROD*** re-enters through the windows.)*

HILDA. We'd better not touch it, then.

MARTIN. I've already touched it.

HILDA. That's different, you had to touch it.

ROD. Touch what?

DOROTHY. That.

ROD. What's that, then?

MARTIN. It's what the kid was carrying. I took it off him.

HILDA. We were saying, it could be a gun.

MARTIN. I don't think it's a gun. Bit long for a gun, isn't it?

ROD. Might be a rifle.

MARTIN. Bit short for a rifle, surely?

ROD. Modified sniper rifle, possibly.

HILDA. *(impressed)* Oh.

MARTIN. *(impressed)* Really?

DOROTHY. *(impressed)* Goodness.

ROD. There's dozens of them. The country's flooded with them. Eastern Europe. Never should have torn down the Iron Curtain. Biggest mistake we ever made. Best not touch it. Be on the safe side.

HILDA. Could it go off, then?

ROD. *(darkly)* In the right hands, it could blow your head off. I'm Rod by the way, from number nine. How do you do?

MARTIN. *(shaking his hand)* How do you do? Martin. This is my sister, Hilda.

HILDA. Hallo.

ROD. Pleased to meet you. Just moved in, have you?

MARTIN. Yes, a few days ago.

ROD. Yes, I saw you yesterday, didn't I? Welcome to the neighbourhood. *(He laughs dryly)*

DOROTHY. What a welcome, then? First day, you get assaulted.

ROD. Par for the course round here. Take my tip, friend, you'll get a fence put up.

HILDA. Oh. Do we really need one?

ROD. They'll be walking in and out of here all day long, otherwise. Riff-raff and vermin...

DOROTHY. At night specially.

MARTIN. Yes, well, we'll consider a fence, won't we, Hilda?

ROD. I mean what have you got at the moment separating you from that field? Just a ditch, isn't it? With a couple of marker posts. Anyone could jump that, easily. In and out in a second.

DOROTHY. They'll have your gnome, quick as a flash.

MARTIN. Sorry?

DOROTHY. Your garden gnome there. You're lucky the kid didn't make off with him.

HILDA. Oh, no, not Monty. They can't take Monty. He's Martin's pride and joy.

ROD. They'll take anything that moves.

HILDA. *(smiling)* Not that he moves, of course.

MARTIN. Only at night-times. He's been known to creep around at night.

(**DOROTHY** *and* **ROD** *stare at him blankly.* **MARTIN** *laughs to help indicate he's joking.*)

HILDA. Oh, Martin, really. Him and his jokes …

ROD. Oh, right … *(He laughs)*

DOROTHY. Oh, yes … *(She laughs)* At night. That's a good one.

HILDA. Don't mind us, we're both completely mad.

MARTIN. Speak for yourself. *(He laughs)*

(They all laugh this time, starting to get the hang of it.)

HILDA. *(wiping her eyes)* Oh, dear. It gets madder by the minute.

ROD. Ah well, it's only being mad that keeps you sane, isn't it?

DOROTHY. I love what you've done to the room, by the way.

HILDA. Do you? Thank you …

DOROTHY. Did you get somebody to do it? You know, design it?

HILDA. No, just us.

MARTIN. All Hilda, this. I can't take credit for this.

DOROTHY. Well, she's very talented. You've got an eye, Hilda. Beautiful, isn't it, Rod?

ROD. Yes, nice green. I like the green.

MARTIN. All Hilda …

HILDA. *(enjoying this, if a trifle embarrassed)* Now, I'm sure we're all dying for a cup of tea, aren't we? *(Moving off)* I've laid everything out in the dining room …

DOROTHY. *(making to follow her)* I'll give you a hand, Hilda …

HILDA. No, it's alright I—

DOROTHY. I'd love to have a little look round. See what you've done with the rest of the place …

(**HILDA** *and* **DOROTHY** *go off.*)

HILDA. *(as they go)* Yes, of course. We're still getting sorted out. It's all a dreadful mess …

(*Slight pause. As the two men are left alone.*)

ROD. No, take my tip, a fence. First thing you need.

MARTIN. You think so?

ROD. If you want to feel secure, you and your sister.

MARTIN. Well …

ROD. I mean, that's the reason everyone else has got a fence. They feel vulnerable. Even I've got a fence.

MARTIN. Really?

ROD. And I was in the security service.

MARTIN. Were you?

ROD. I can handle myself. Twenty-five years. Before that, the army. Not much frightens me, mate. But even I've got myself a fence. First rule of security, get yourself a fence.

MARTIN. Well, my sister was worried about losing the view. The vista.

ROD. Suit yourself. It's either a fence or a dozen yobbos coming up the hill intent on vandalising the place.

MARTIN. As bad as that?

ROD. That estate down there, the Councillor Mountjoy Estate, it's a cesspit. All the local scum gathered down there. Drugs, violence … incest.

MARTIN. Goodness!

ROD. Go down and have a look at it if you want. Only during the daytime, mind you. It'll turn your stomach. Streets coated in vomit, blood, graffiti and worse … Half the doors hanging off, windows broken, boarded up … Street lights vandalised … Sodom and Gomorrah.

MARTIN. You'd think the police would have stepped in, wouldn't you …

ROD. The police? Forget them. It's a no-go zone. Won't get a copper venturing in there after dark. Not even in full riot gear. I have a friend in the force and he tells me that, day to day, the police are hanging on by a whisker … by that much … It's not just here, mark you. It's nation-wide. One breath of wind – anarchy! That's a serving police officer told me that. He says that lately his chief super, his chief superintendant this is, he's taken to cowering under his office desk. Anyone knocks he shouts out, "Whatever it is, I don't want to know!"

MARTIN. That's unbelievable!

(The doorbell rings.)

Ah, I think that may be someone …

ROD. *(now fully warmed up)* No, they're fighting a losing battle, poor sods. You can't help but feel sorry for them, the police. It's every man for himself, mate. First thing you need to do is get yourself a fence.

MARTIN. Right. I must just see who –

ROD. It doesn't need to be a solid fence. I mean, your sister can still enjoy her vista. No, what you need is reinforced chain link. Industrial strength. Eight feet high. No lower. Razor wire on the top. You're welcome to come and have a look at mine. I'll chain the dog up, first.

MARTIN. Dog?

*(**HILDA** and **DOROTHY** return with four cups of tea between them.)*

ROD. Oh, that's another thing. You might consider getting yourself a dog as well. They're reassuring.

HILDA. Are we talking about dogs? I'd love a little doggie. I keep trying to talk Martin into having one. We brought you both a cup. Here, Martin, that's yours. Dorothy's got yours, Rod. She says she knows how you like it.

DOROTHY. I should do by now. Here we are, Rod. Sugared as you like it.

ROD. Ta.

HILDA. Oh, there's someone else arrived, Martin.

MARTIN. *(making to move)* Oh, right, I'll …

HILDA. No, it's alright. No rush. He's in the – little boys' room.

ROD. Who is it?

DOROTHY. It's Gareth.

ROD. Oh, him. *(Significantly)* Has he brought her with him?

DOROTHY. *(likewise)* No, he's on his own.

ROD. Good.

DOROTHY. Thankfully. She's following on later. *(Explaining to the others)* Mr and Mrs Janner from number eight.

HILDA. He seems very nice.

DOROTHY. Yes, <u>he</u>'s very nice.

ROD. <u>He</u>'s nice enough. Good cup of tea.

HILDA. Thank you.

*(Pause. They drink. Conversation appears to have dried up temporarily. **ROD** contemplates the nibbles.)*

DOROTHY. Yes, it is a good cup of tea.

HILDA. Thank you. Yes, help yourself, Rod, they're there to be eaten.

*(**ROD** tries one of the nibbles. He decides against eating any more.)*

Dorothy was explaining to me, Martin, the reason we're the only ones who don't have a fence is that old Mrs Beadie who was here before refused to have one …

DOROTHY. No, that's right, she did.

ROD. We tried persuading her …

DOROTHY. She had an open house. Kids wandering in and out all day. Shouting, laughing, swearing, smoking …

HILDA. 'dear …

DOROTHY. She used to give them fruit juice and buns …

MARTIN. Buns?

ROD. *(shaking his head)* She was lucky to be alive, that's all I can say.

DOROTHY. Well, she's not now. She died peacefully in her bed. Just upstairs there. Sorry, you're not superstitious are you, either of you?

HILDA. No. Not in that way, anyway. We've nothing at all to fear. Not from the Other Side.

MARTIN. Perhaps that's why that kid was climbing in here just now. In search of buns? *(He laughs)*

DOROTHY. What, with a rifle?

MARTIN. We don't know it's a rifle. Not necessarily.

(They all stare at the case.)

HILDA. I'm dying to look, see what it is.

ROD. I wouldn't advise it. Leave your fingerprints on there, knowing them they'll probably charge you with nicking it.

HILDA. They wouldn't do that, surely?

ROD. Oh, you've no idea. I had this hedge trimmer, you remember – shall I tell them about my hedge trimmer? Shall I tell them, Dorothy?

DOROTHY. Oh yes, do. Tell them about your hedge trimmer, Rod … He bought this hedge trimmer, you see …

ROD. I bought this hedge trimmer …

DOROTHY. Brand new …

ROD. Brand new, mark you …

DOROTHY. He hadn't had it a week …

ROD. Less than a week …

(GARETH Janner, *a man in his forties, has entered. He has a cup of tea.)*

GARETH. Hallo, everyone.

HILDA. Hallo, come in, Gareth – you don't mind me calling you Gareth, do you?

GARETH. No, not at all. Helped myself to a cup of tea, hope you don't mind?

ROD. Hallo, Gareth. Just telling them about my hedge trimmer …

GARETH. Oh, that. Right. Carry on. *(To* **MARTIN***)* Hallo. I'm Gareth.

MARTIN. Martin. Hallo. Her brother.

DOROTHY. Hallo, Gareth.

GARETH. Hi, Dorothy.

DOROTHY. Go on, Rod. He bought this brand new hedge trimmer, you see. Hadn't had it a week, had you, Rod?

ROD. Less than a week. I was trimming the front hedge …

DOROTHY. He's got this little bit of a hedge, you see. He was calmly trimming away …

GARETH. Oh yes, that's right, I remember. You turned round for ten minutes, didn't you?

ROD. Ten minutes, that's all it was…

DOROTHY. Just to make himself a cup of tea …

GARETH. This bloke walks in through his front gate …

DOROTHY. Cool as you like …

ROD. Cool as you like, barefaced … and he walks off with it …

GARETH. He calmly walks off with it.

MARTIN. Heavens!

HILDA. Gracious!

DOROTHY. Broad daylight. But, you see, Rod recognised him, didn't you, Rod?

ROD. I'd seen him around from the Mountjoy Estate …

GARETH. He was from the Estate …

MARTIN. Aha!

ROD. And I thought, he's not getting away with that, no way is he getting away with that …

DOROTHY. He didn't know Rod.

MARTIN. What did you do, report him?

ROD. I certainly did. Went straight down to the police station, gave them full description, everything short of the bloke's DNA and fingerprints. All they had to do was stroll down there and nick him. But instead, what happens?

DOROTHY. He waited days, didn't you, days …

ROD. Days and days …

DOROTHY. While all the police did was fill in forms.

GARETH. So in the end, what did he do? You went down there yourself, didn't you?

ROD. In sheer frustration. I walked straight into this bloke's house …

DOROTHY. Rod knew where he lived, you see. He walked straight in there without knocking …

ROD. And I said to him, "Oy, you, sunshine, what have you done with my hedge trimmer?"

DOROTHY. What have you done with it?

GARETH. He's acting all innocent like, isn't he?

ROD. Sitting there calm as you like, reading the evening paper.

GARETH. Reading the paper, wasn't he?

DOROTHY. So he'd had enough, by now, hadn't you, Rod?

ROD. I started turning the place over, you know, gently to start with, I'm looking in all his cupboards and under his furniture and finally …

GARETH. He tips this bloke out of his chair, don't you…?

ROD. Straight out of the chair, on the floor, flat on his face …

DOROTHY. Flat on his face …

ROD. And there it is, my hedge trimmer. Stashed underneath it …

GARETH. Under his chair …

DOROTHY. Where this bloke's hiding it.

MARTIN. What happened then?

HILDA. What did you do then?

ROD. I went back home and I finished off my hedge, didn't I?

MARTIN. Good for you!

HILDA. Well done.

GARETH. No, well … until … tell him the other bit, Rod …

DOROTHY. Tell them the rest of it, Rod … Later on, Rod gets this visit …

GARETH. From the police, wasn't it …?

ROD. Couple of them. To tell me there's been a complaint from this bloke. Damage to his property, physical assault …

DOROTHY. Can you believe this? Can you believe this?

ROD. Threatening to charge me. I said hang on. He stole my hedge trimmer, that's what started it.

GARETH. He started it.

ROD. They said, where is it now, then? I said, it's in my shed hanging up where it belongs. And they said, how do you know it's yours? I said, I saw him nicking it less than a week ago. They said, have you got proof of that? I said, how many more times, I saw him. They said, well, he denies it. And I said, well, he would do, wouldn't he? And they said, then it's his word against yours, isn't it? You can't go around taking the law in your own hands, that's breaking the law. I said, what? I said, <u>what</u>? They said, that hedge trimmer was reported stolen four days ago and we've still got it down here as an unsolved crime, it's still officially stolen until it's been officially recovered. And what's more, if you're not careful, if we find your fingerprints on it, we'll have you for receiving stolen property, as well. I mean, where's the justice? Where's the justice?

MARTIN. What happened to the hedge trimmer?

ROD. Still at the police station, isn't it? Officially being held as evidence. Except I'm sure one of those bastards is trimming his own hedge with it. No, don't you get me started on the law.

DOROTHY. Don't get him started …

GARETH. You'll never stop him, once he gets started.

HILDA. Well. I'm appalled. Enough to make you lose trust, isn't it?

MARTIN. Certainly is.

(A sober moment of reflection.)

DOROTHY. Where's Amy, Gareth? She's very late.

GARETH. *(awkwardly)* Yes, well … she's possibly been held up. I don't know.

DOROTHY. She is coming, though?

GARETH. Oh, yes, probably. She said she was.

DOROTHY. Is her back any better?

GARETH. *(uncomfortably)* No. Not a lot.

DOROTHY. She's still undergoing treatment, then?

GARETH. Yes.

HILDA. I've had back trouble … *(To* **MARTIN***)* Haven't I?

MARTIN. You certainly have.

DOROTHY. She's still having it done by the man at number thirteen, is she?

GARETH. No, she's not seeing him any more. She's moved on …

DOROTHY. Trying someone else, is she?

GARETH. Apparently.

DOROTHY. Well, I hope she'll get someone to straighten her out eventually, Gareth. For your sake.

GARETH. *(suddenly, moving to the door)* Would you mind if I helped myself to another cup of tea?

HILDA. *(making to go with him)* No, of course. The pot may need topping up. Let me.

GARETH. No, I'm sorry, I didn't mean to …

MARTIN. *(intercepting her)* No I'll go, Hilda … Stay there. I'll come with you, Gareth. If we're starting on about medical conditions, leave it to the women-folk. Best off out of it, aren't we …? *(He laughs)*

(GARETH *gives a sickly smile and he and* **MARTIN** *go off to the kitchen.)*

(ROD, *left alone with the women, appears awkward.)*

(A pause.)

HILDA. Well, looking at the time, I don't think anyone else is coming, do you?

DOROTHY. I think most people, round here, you know, they're all very busy. This time of year, you know. It's alright for people like us, Rod, isn't it? Being retired.

ROD. I'm still kept busy.

DOROTHY. And then poor Gareth, of course, being made redundant. Mind you, he keeps busy, doesn't he?

ROD. He does.

DOROTHY. In that shed of his.

ROD. Oh, yes …

HILDA. What does he get up to in his shed, then?

DOROTHY. Oh, all sorts of things. He's an engineer, isn't he?

ROD. He was.

DOROTHY. Wonderful with his hands. Turn them to anything. His hands. Metal work. Woodwork. You name it. He did a wonderful job on my hanging baskets, didn't he, Rod?

ROD. Skilled craftsman. On the scrap heap. Years before his time. Crying shame. Death of British industry.

HILDA. Same all over.

DOROTHY. Crying shame.

(Silence.)

HILDA. This man at number thirteen. Is he good with backs?

DOROTHY. They say he is. I've never tried him. Gareth's wife, Amy, she swears by him. She always comes out of there smiling, anyway.

HILDA. Really?

ROD. Look, I think I'll – just join them out there, if you'll excuse me. *(Indicating the plate of uneaten nibbles)* Very nice … unusual …

HILDA. Well, help yourself, there's masses more out there.

*(**ROD** goes out to the kitchen.)*

I made enough for dozens. I don't know what we're going to do with them. I hate waste, don't you?

DOROTHY. Oh, yes.

(The doorbell rings.)

HILDA. Oh, more people. It's alright. Martin'll let them in. Sorry, you were saying, Dorothy? Number thirteen?

DOROTHY. Yes, his name's Ruderbeck. Ralph Ruderbeck. He's a Swiss. Apparently. Foreign, anyway.

HILDA. A therapist, is he?

DOROTHY. Of sorts. Amy's been seeing him for ages. Quite openly. She doesn't care who knows it, either. It's him I feel sorry for. Making Gareth look … Her own husband. She's demeaned him.

HILDA. Poor man.

DOROTHY. Still, as you heard, she's moved on since him. Gradually working her way round Bluebell Hill. Better watch – oh, no, he's only your brother, isn't he? I was forgetting.

HILDA. *(smiling at the idea)* He'd better not! Who's she with now, do we know?

DOROTHY. Well, according to Della at number seven, Mrs Cable … She's at it with him … *(Mouthing, silently)* … next door.

HILDA. *(not hearing her)* Sorry?

DOROTHY. Him, next door. Next door to you. Mr Bradley. Luther Bradley.

HILDA. Oh.

DOROTHY. Hark at me gossiping on. That's what fifteen years on a local paper does for you.

HILDA. Were you? Were you really?

DOROTHY. Fifteen years on *The Advertiser*. Before it folded. Old habits die hard. Still have the nose for a good story.

HILDA. Fascinating. No, I mean, as you say, what can it be like for him? For her husband, poor man. If she's –

DOROTHY. He should have done something ages ago. Taken a stand. But Gareth's not the type.

HILDA. I wonder why she married him?

DOROTHY. Before my time. Apparently on the rebound from someone else, by all accounts. She'd never have looked at him, otherwise. Let's face it, he's not much of a catch is Gareth.

HILDA. Poor man.

DOROTHY. Now, if it had been Rod there, he'd never have stood for it. Not for a minute. Gone round and sorted the bloke out. Sorted her out as well, most like.

HILDA. Was he ever married, do you know? Rod?

DOROTHY. Yes. Only they say she … his wife … *(Confidentially)* … ran away.

HILDA. Ran away?

DOROTHY. So they say.

HILDA. Perhaps he sorted her out.

DOROTHY. Wouldn't put it past him. I mean, he's nice enough, everyday, don't get me wrong. But then he gets this look in his eyes. Just occasionally.

HILDA. Yes?

DOROTHY. You should see him talking to his dog sometimes. Terrified of him, she is.

*(**AMY** enters, attractive, in her mid thirties. From the reputation that has preceded her, she does not disappoint.)*

AMY. Hallo, mind if I join you?

DOROTHY. Oh hallo, Amy. This is Amy, Hilda, I was telling you all about.

HILDA. Oh, yes. Nice to meet you, Amy. Thank you for coming.

AMY. Sorry I'm a bit late. Typical. I got held up. Thank God, I arrived with a couple of others so at least I'm not the last.

HILDA. I think your husband's in the dining room, Amy. If you're looking for him.

AMY. *(offhandedly)* Not specially, no. I stuck my head in there briefly.

HILDA. Are they alright in there?

AMY. Oh, yes. They're having a high old time. Rod Trusser's keeping them entertained with tales of hedge trimmers ...

HILDA. Oh, yes! What a story! It's unbelievable, isn't it?

AMY. Yes, it is, isn't it? It improves every time with the telling. Sorry was I interrupting – ?

HILDA. No, not at all. Do sit down, Amy. Would you like some tea?

AMY. No, thanks, that's OK. Your – Martin, is it? – your husband's bringing me some.

HILDA. No, he's my brother. Martin's my brother.

AMY. Oh, sorry. He's your brother?

HILDA. I don't have a husband.

AMY. *(smiling)* Lucky you. Hallo, Dorothy.

DOROTHY. *(slightly stiffly)* Hallo, Amy.

AMY. Been filling Hilda in with all the gossip then, have you?

DOROTHY. A little.

AMY. I bet you have. So how's it all going, Hilda? Settling in OK?

HILDA. Yes, we've been here, well, nearly two months, on and off. Popping in on odd days, you know. We've only moved in properly in the last week.

AMY. Poor you. I don't envy you. Moving house is always murder, isn't it? What is it they say about it? It's one of the most traumatic things that can happen to most people in their entire lives. I don't know what the others are. Getting married and losing your virginity, probably.

(She laughs. **DOROTHY** *doesn't.)*

HILDA. *(smiling frostily)* Yes, we're gradually getting straight. Still masses more to do, of course.

AMY. Yes, I can see. *(Looking around)* Masses. This room for a kick off. God! This wallpaper for a start. I ask you, how anyone could bear to live with this day after day for any length of ...

(Slight pause.)

(realising) Whoops.

HILDA. *(icily)* My brother finished decorating it yesterday.

AMY. It's simply stunning! Congratulations!

HILDA. *(slightly tensely)* Thank you. I'm particularly fond of this paper. It was quite expensive, actually.

AMY. Wow!

DOROTHY. As I said, I think it's quite beautiful, Hilda. It shows magnificent taste.

AMY. Yes. *(Slight pause)* Sorry to ask – but the choice of paintwork, that's yours, too? *(A slight pause)* Yep. Thought it was. Inspired. Great choice. Brilliant. Green. *(Slight pause. Singing)* Isn't it a lovely day, to be caught in the rain ...?

(Silence.)

*(***MARTIN** *enters with a cup of tea for* **AMY***.)*

MARTIN. Sorry, Amy, I'd have been a bit quicker, only ...

AMY. Thank you.

(MARTIN gives her the tea. The silence between the women continues.)

MARTIN. ... I had to wait till Rod had finished his story again ... Well, how are things in here? Having a good time then?

(Silence. MARTIN becomes aware that things aren't going too well.)

(DOROTHY and HILDA maintain their frozen silence.)

DOROTHY. *(rising suddenly)* Excuse me, I must just – have that little peek at the bedrooms, if I may, Hilda?

HILDA. *(rising)* Yes, of course, Dorothy. I'll show you round...

DOROTHY. Oh, lovely. I'm dying to see what you've done upstairs...

(DOROTHY and HILDA go out to the hall.)

AMY. *(cheerfully)* I think your sister and I may have just got off on the wrong foot,

MARTIN. Oh, dear. Why's that?

AMY. I'm afraid I was rather rude about her choice of colour scheme.

MARTIN. Oh yes, that would do it. Hilda's quite sensitive in that department. *(Smiling)* As I know to my cost over the years.

AMY. That's me, I'm afraid. What I lack in tact, I make up for in honesty. Which makes a refreshing change from most of the people round here on this narrow-minded, middle-class, fucking little estate.

MARTIN. I warn you, you certainly won't get on any better with her if you start using language like that in front of her.

AMY. What, middle-class, you mean? I do beg your pardon.

(MARTIN finds this amusing.)

Sorry. I take it you don't share her views on wallpaper.

MARTIN. She and I have occasionally begged to differ in the past. These days I tend to settle for the quiet life.

AMY. Or so-called bad language? Do you share her views on that?

MARTIN. No, not really. I've been known to use it occasionally myself. Under my breath and under stress. Struggling to put up this sodding wallpaper for one ...

(**AMY** *laughs.*)

But I try not to swear too often. I think on the whole, it's usually the symptom of a somewhat inadequate vocabulary. I mean, there's so many beautiful words one can use. Why settle for an ugly one?

AMY. Yes. You're right. There are. Beautiful words. Meringue. That's a pretty word.

MARTIN. Right. Next time I hit my thumb with the hammer I'll try that. Oh, meringues!

AMY. M words are generally nice. Mellifluous. Melodic ... (*Looking out of the window, with a cry of delight*) Oh, look out here, I can't believe it. There's a gnome. A garden gnome. That surely must have been left over from old Mrs ...? No? Thank God I didn't spot it whilst your sister was here. Imagine if I'd made mock of her gnome ...?

MARTIN. No, he's mine, actually. He belongs to me.

AMY. Your gnome?

MARTIN. 'fraid so. I've had him since I was a kid. He was a birthday present. A stupid birthday present for a five-year-old ... but ...

AMY. From your parents? Did your parents give him to you?

MARTIN. My mother. Last birthday present she gave me, actually. Before she died. He's called Monty, by the way. Short for Montmorency.

AMY. That's nice. Another M word. (*smiling*) Then there's Martin, of course.

MARTIN. Martin Massie. Two of them.

AMY. Two? That's unfair.

MARTIN. Amy.

AMY. A – words? Not so good. A's. Mostly negatives. Awful.
Abominable. Anti-social … Aggressive …

MARTIN. Attractive?

AMY. … appalling …

MARTIN. … angelic …

AMY. … altogether atrocious … !

MARTIN. *(rapidly)* … agreeable … appealing … alluring …
awesome … adorable … amazing … audacious …
august … appetising … amusing … altruistic …
astounding … affecting … adventurous … admirable …

AMY. *(holding up hands in defeat)* OK. OK. You win.

MARTIN. I do a lot of crosswords …

AMY. *(smiling)* Right. I really must do some serious work on
my vocabulary.

MARTIN. *(smiling)* Absolutely.

*(A silence. **AMY** smiles at him. **MARTIN** smiles back at
her. The doorbell rings. Neither registers it.)*

AMY. Well, you're full of surprises, aren't you, Mr – Martin –
Massie.

MARTIN. *(nodding)* Mmm.

(They look at each other.)

*(Love at first sight might be nothing new for **AMY** but for
MARTIN it is very much the first time.)*

*(**HILDA** enters with **MAGDA**, in her 20s and at present
very distraught.)*

HILDA. Martin, this is Magda from next door. She's – she's
in a bit of a state …

MARTIN. What on earth's wrong?

HILDA. Her husband isn't back from work yet. She's all on
her own next door and –

MARTIN. Come and sit down, Magda. What's the problem?

(**MAGDA** *shoots* **AMY** *a look.*)

You know Amy, of course …?

AMY. *(moving to the door)* Excuse me, I'll just …

(**AMY** *goes out.* **MARTIN** *is slightly puzzled.* **HILDA** *sits* **MAGDA** *on the sofa.*)

HILDA. *(shooing* **MARTIN** *from the room)* It's alright, Martin. Leave this to me. It may be – it might be – *(Mouthing to him)* it might be a – a woman's thing …

MARTIN. Oh, right. One of those. Right. *(He hurries out)*

HILDA. *(gently, as soon as he has gone)* Now, tell me. You can tell me, dear. What's the problem? You can tell me. I'm very broad-minded.

MAGDA. I do apologise – bothering you with all – when you've got a house full of – I'm sorry – It's just so awful. It's Ethan, you see –

HILDA. Ethan? Who's Ethan?

MAGDA. One of my students – he's brilliant – he's just so sensitive and talented – he's brilliant. I'm a music teacher, you see – woodwind – and I give private lessons after school. Next door. And one of my students has just been attacked and robbed. On his way home from a lesson. His father's just phoned me in a terrible state. It happened about an hour ago. I let Ethan leave by the back way, as always, and he was apparently climbing the fence and … this man came from nowhere. Probably some terrible paedophile – and he grabbed hold of Ethan. And they struggled and Ethan managed to escape. Only the man made off with his instrument.

(As **MAGDA** *is speaking,* **HILDA**'s *eyes have been sliding round to look at the music case.*)

HILDA. *(the truth dawning)* I see. I see. This instrument. Can you describe it?

MAGDA. It's an ordinary student clarinet in an old case. A standard B flat clarinet. Second hand. Not really worth

much. I don't know why the man took it, it's of no use
to him …

HILDA. *(revealing the case)* Is this it? Is this the one?

MAGDA. Oh! Oh! Oh! How did you – ? *(Opening the case
and examining its contents briefly)* Yes, it's all here, it's
definitely his! *(Overjoyed)* Oh thank you, thank you!
You're an angel! A guardian angel! Thank you!

*(MAGDA kisses a bewildered HILDA impetuously on both
cheeks.)*

Bless you. I don't know how you found it! But this will
make him so happy. There is a God! There is a God,
after all. Thank you! May I take it to him?

HILDA. Yes, of course. If it belongs to him …

MAGDA. Thank you. I'll ring him first! I'll give Ethan a call.
He'll just be so happy, you've no idea! See you soon.

(MAGDA rushes out to the front door.)

HILDA. Oh, dear. Oh, dear, oh dear. *(As she goes, calling)*
Martin! Martin, dear …

*(As HILDA slowly goes out to the kitchen, music as the
lights fade to:)*

Scene Two

(The same, a few days later.)

(Late afternoon. It gradually grows dark through the scene.)

*(**LUTHER** Bradley, **MAGDA**'s husband, in his late thirties, is standing by the window impatiently waiting.)*

*(In a moment, **HILDA** enters with **MARTIN**.)*

HILDA. This is Mr Bradley, Martin. I'll leave you both. Excuse me.

*(**HILDA** goes out again.)*

MARTIN. *(prepared for trouble)* Good afternoon. What can I do for you, Mr Bradley? I'm afraid I don't have a lot of time, we have an important meeting here in a minute.

LUTHER. Oh, yes. This so-called Neighbourhood Watch meeting you've called. I hope you weren't expecting my wife and I to attend?

MARTIN. That's entirely up to you, Mr Bradley. An invitation was extended next door at number five to you and to Mrs Bradley, as indeed has one to everybody at Bluebell Hill. Now, I repeat, what can I do for you?

LUTHER. I think you know why I'm here, Mr Massie. It's concerning your assault on a child the other day, putting it briefly.

MARTIN. I beg your pardon, my assault on a <u>child</u>?

LUTHER. The young person whom you set upon and robbed whilst innocently on his way home ...

MARTIN. I cannot believe I am hearing this. What on earth are you talking about?

LUTHER. Ethan Dudgeon, the young person whom you set upon and robbed whilst innocently on his way home from a music lesson with my wife. Whom you robbed, making off with his rightful property ...

MARTIN. I presume you're referring to the same youth, the one I legitimately apprehended whilst illegally climbing over my wall –

LUTHER. – <u>our</u> wall – it's a party wall –

MARTIN. Granted – into <u>my</u> garden, caught *flagrante delicto* in the act of illegal trespass. Carrying what appeared to be, judging from his furtive and secretive behaviour, stolen property? That innocent child?

LUTHER. Oh, come off it, Mr Massie, that is total bollocks and you know it –

MARTIN. That was how it appeared to me in the heat of that moment in time.

LUTHER. Did you even ask him what he was doing there, Mr Massie?

MARTIN. I didn't get a chance to, did I? He kicked me in the leg! If I was mistaken, as it appears I may have been, then as I said to you on the phone, I am fully prepared to apologise to all parties.

LUTHER. I think this is beyond a mere apology, Mr Massie.

MARTIN. Well, that's all you're getting, I'm sorry.

LUTHER. Since you and I spoke on the phone, I have consulted with the lad's distraught father, Mr Dudgeon, and we are both of the opinion that we are entitled to some compensation.

MARTIN. *(incredulously)* Compensation? Are we talking about <u>financial</u> compensation?

LUTHER. Indeed we are. That boy, Ethan, is a sensitive child. He has undergone traumatic distress and, as a result, he can no longer face another music lesson and he's selling his clarinet. His family are heartbroken. Their dreams for their only son who showed such potential talent, whose future career as a clarinet player knew no boundaries, have been dashed. According to my wife, Magda, Ethan stood a fair chance of ending up in the London Symphony Orchestra. As for her, you appreciate because of the cancelled lessons, she has undergone a considerable loss of income and as a consequence, she's been forced to lie down with the curtains drawn in a darkened room.

MARTIN. Well, I'm very sorry to hear that. My sympathy goes out to all concerned.

(The front doorbell rings. They ignore it.)

LUTHER. I should warn you that Mr Dudgeon and I are prepared, if it comes to it, to have recourse to the law, Mr Massie.

MARTIN. Well, I should certainly do that, Mr Bradley, if I were you. As my late father would have put it, I eagerly look forward to hearing from your solicitors, Messrs. Balderdash, Bluster and Bunkum.

LUTHER. If that's the way you want it. We shall see, won't we?

MARTIN. We shall indeed. Oh, by the way, when you next have occasion to speak to Barry Dudgeon, say two words to him from me, will you? Hedge trimmer!

LUTHER. What?

MARTIN. Just say that. Hedge trimmer. I've been doing my research, Mr Bradley.

LUTHER. *(mystified)* Hedge trimmer?

(HILDA shows in MAGDA who enters nervously. HILDA hovers in the doorway.)

HILDA. I'm so sorry to interrupt, Martin, but Mrs Bradley was anxious to have a word with you.

LUTHER. *(evidently angry to see her)* What are you doing here, Magda? I told you to stay at home.

MARTIN. Please do come in, Magda. If I may call you Magda?

MAGDA. *(distraught)* Luther, we mustn't keep on with this, we really mustn't –

LUTHER. *(sharply)* Magda, I told you to keep out of this!

(MAGDA flinches.)

HILDA. I'd prefer it if you didn't shout at your wife, Mr Bradley. Not in our house.

(A silence.)

MAGDA. The only one who is going to lose out in all this, is Ethan. I'm thinking of Ethan. What's all this going to do to him? It'll ruin his future.

MARTIN. I understand that's already ruined.

MAGDA. What?

MARTIN. According to your husband, he can no longer face another music lesson and he's selling his clarinet.

MAGDA. That's rubbish. *(To* **LUTHER***)* Who said that? Who told you that?

LUTHER. *(muttering)* According to Barry Dudgeon …

MAGDA. Oh, that man … Anyway it isn't his to sell. It isn't even his instrument …

MARTIN. It isn't?

MAGDA. Ethan could never have afforded one. Not even a cheap one. His father would never … *(She tails off)*

LUTHER. Then where did he get it?

MAGDA. *(blurting it out)* Alright! It cost seventy-nine pounds plus postage from the internet and I bought it for him with my own money!

(A pause.)

LUTHER. *(slowly)* You did what?

MAGDA. I bought it for him. I didn't tell you because …

LUTHER. You spent seventy-nine pounds of our money on that …? Of our money…?

MAGDA. … no, of <u>my</u> money, Luther. It was my money …

LUTHER. … seventy-nine pounds …?

MAGDA. … he needed one so he could practise. He asked his father but Dudgeon's such a terrible man, he wouldn't – even – rent him one –

MARTIN. Aha! Now we're hearing it. Terrible man. His own father, the lad's own distraught father, and he wouldn't even bring himself to buy the lad a cut-price clarinet …

MAGDA. He could have afforded it, if he'd wanted to. Instead he spent all his money on drink and drugs and – pigeon food ...

LUTHER. Pigeon food?

MAGDA. He said that sort of music was middle class rubbish – or some such nonsense. No, it's Ethan we should feel sorry for. He's the one losing out. His father won't let him come for any more lessons. He refuses to let him.

MARTIN. From the sound of the man, I'm amazed he was even prepared to pay for them in the first place ...

(He stops at the sight of MAGDA's *guilty expression.)*

Sorry.

MAGDA. *(staring at her feet)* Well, I ...

LUTHER. I don't believe it. Magda, you gave that boy free lessons as well? On top of a complimentary clarinet?

MAGDA. Luther, you've no idea! A boy from a background like that –

LUTHER. What else did you give him, for Christ's sake?

MAGDA. If you're a teacher, you pray to find a natural talent like that once in a lifetime. Natural ... He was a natural –

LUTHER. *(snapping)* And you're a natural gullible idiot!

(A brief silence. Even LUTHER *realises he may have gone too far. In public at least.)*

HILDA. We'll have to ask you to leave now, Mr Bradley. This room is required for a meeting.

LUTHER. We're going, don't worry. Come along, Magda.

MAGDA. I think I'll stay.

LUTHER. What?

MAGDA. I said, I'll stay for this meeting. There may be things that concern us.

*(*LUTHER *stares at her. He looks as if he might hit her.)*

HILDA. You'll be most welcome to stay, Magda. Won't she, Martin?

MARTIN. Oh, yes. Most welcome.

LUTHER. *(moving to the door)* This isn't the end of this business. I'm phoning Mr Dudgeon now. I'm sure he will wish to take this matter on from here.

MARTIN. Give him my regards. Don't forget to mention the hedge trimmer, will you?

LUTHER. *(as he goes, muttering)* What's all this about a bloody hedge trimmer?

*(**LUTHER** goes out.)*

MARTIN. I'll see you off the premises, Mr Bradley. *(He moves to follow **LUTHER**)*

HILDA. *(as **MARTIN** passes)* Well done, Martin.

*(**MARTIN** goes out.)*

*(To **MAGDA**)* I think that was very brave of you. Standing up to him.

MAGDA. He's not … Luther's not – usually … anyway, not in front of other people … he's … It's just I feel so strongly … I really do ….

HILDA. *(taking her hand)* In this life, you must always stand up for things you believe in, Magda. Even if bigger and stronger people don't always agree with you. You did right.

MAGDA. Thank you.

*(**HILDA** continues to hold **MAGDA**'s hand until **MAGDA** rather self-consciously withdraws it.)*

Actually, I didn't say – not in front of Luther – but I gave Ethan permission to take the short cut. I mean when old Mrs Beadie was here, it wasn't a problem, but – when you and your brother – I should have said to you – only I didn't think. It's all entirely my fault.

HILDA. Not to worry.

MAGDA. It was just easier for Ethan going that way. Otherwise he has to walk all the way round, crossing that busy ring road. I always used to worry.

HILDA. Trust my brother. He'll sort it out. He's strong. He has inner strength.

MAGDA. Yes, I'm sure he has.

(**MARTIN** *appears in the hall doorway.*)

MARTIN. Are we alright to bring them in then, Hilda? There's a few of them arrived, anyway.

HILDA. Oh, yes.

MARTIN. *(calling back through the doorway)* Would you care to come in, please?

(**MARTIN** *ushers* **ROD, DOROTHY** *and* **GARETH** *in. General greetings between the new arrivals and* **HILDA** *and* **MAGDA**. *They all seat themselves on the sofas.*)

(*A brief silence.*)

MARTIN. Well, this appears to be it. The usual suspects, I think.

(**ROD** *shakes his head disgustedly.*)

First of all. For those of you I haven't managed to contact in time, my apologies – a bit of bad news, I'm afraid. I had a call earlier from police sergeant Rawlings who is apparently our local liaison officer in charge of advising on the setting up of neighbourhood watch schemes ... Unfortunately, he tells me, owing to pressure of work – vital police work – and, of course, due to the recent cut-backs .. they couldn't regrettably spare anyone to come along this evening to advise us ...

DOROTHY. Oh, dear

ROD. *(muttering)* Typical ...

MARTIN. My first instinct was to postpone this meeting altogether, but then I thought, we can set this up for ourselves, surely? After all, what are the police going to tell us? That's fairly predictable, surely? During the day, at all times, exercise vigilance. If you go out, lock your windows and doors. Take note of any suspicious or unusual behaviour, especially regarding strangers.

And at night, organise peaceful patrols. With two or more able-bodied volunteers to do the rounds of the property at intervals, always varying the routine so the villains are never sure when to expect them. If something does occur, and they run into something suspicious, first issue a reasonable challenge. If that is ignored, issue a second reasonable challenge; and then, if necessary, a third one ...

ROD. Providing the bugger hasn't legged it by then ...

MARTIN. Well, in that case we'll have frightened him off, won't we? Mission accomplished! That's a positive result, isn't it? And if it is necessary to apprehend someone, employ only reasonable force in order to subdue him ... With the emphasis on reasonable ...

ROD. Or else the bastard will turn round and sue you ...

GARETH. What if he's armed?

MARTIN. If the suspect turns out be armed, then exercise caution. If it's a knife, keep your distance, if it's a gun, take cover or run like hell. That's probably what they'd advise us to do. It's all common sense really.

GARETH. Where are we going to find these volunteers? Judging from the vast crowds who've come along this evening, this is hardly a pressing issue for most people on Bluebell Hill, is it?

DOROTHY. Apathy. As Rod here's said, time and again, sheer apathy. Well, they'll be sorry, that's all I can say, when it happens to them, they'll all come crying for help, you'll see. Wait till it happens to them.

MAGDA. When what happens to them?

DOROTHY. *(darkly)* Everything. Robbery, violence. Destruction to your property. Personal invasion of your private space. Especially if you're a woman. Some thug in a ski mask, climbing in through your window at night ...

HILDA. Dorothy, don't go on, you're frightening Magda.

DOROTHY. Sorry, love.

MAGDA. No, she's right, it can happen … it can easily happen …

ROD. Oh, yes, easily …

MARTIN. *(firmly)* Well, not round here it won't. Providing we take sensible precautions. No need to be afraid, ladies. Not while you have us.

GARETH. Who's us? That's what I'm asking …

MARTIN. … well, we'll have to organise a vigorous recruiting drive, won't we …?

GARETH. … you, me and him? We're not going to be able to protect you, are we?

MARTIN. Yes, point taken, Gareth. We don't want to start spreading despondency, now do we? Anyone else anything to add? Before we adjourn for tea?

HILDA. I'll put the kettle on… *(She starts to rise)*

DOROTHY. Switch all the lights on, Hilda. Just in case …

MARTIN. Anyone else?

DOROTHY. And don't forget to draw the curtains.

HILDA. I will.

(HILDA goes off to the kitchen momentarily.)

MARTIN. Rod? Anything to add?

ROD. In my opinion we'd stand a better chance if these patrols were armed.

MAGDA. Armed?

ROD. Lightly armed.

MARTIN. How do you mean, Rod, lightly armed?

ROD. Baseball bats. They have their uses. Bloody awful sport but a very useful weapon.

DOROTHY. Oh, dear.

ROD. Go for the knees or elbows. That'll get his attention. That's as good as a challenge and more effective. If you catch anyone red-handed, club him senseless and sort it out later.

MARTIN. Oh no, no, no, Rod, out of the question. The police would never condone that.

ROD. We don't need them.

MARTIN. Sorry?

ROD. You're right. We can do this without the police. They'll be worse than useless as far as we're concerned. I mean, look at it this way. We have a serious shortage of man power at present, right?

GARETH. That's my point.

ROD. Now, has it occurred to you, why that is?

DOROTHY. Apathy.

(HILDA returns from the kitchen.)

HILDA. It's on.

ROD. Now, have you considered this? Perhaps the reason we've got so few attending tonight is because you've announced the police were going to be involved?

MARTIN. I don't quite follow.

ROD. There are a considerable number of people – and this is a tragic reflection of the times we're living in – but it is a fact of life that there are an increasing number who have developed a natural mistrust of the police.

HILDA. Who?

ROD. More widespread than you might imagine.

MARTIN. Who are these people?

ROD. You'd be amazed. A lot of them on this Bluebell Hill. People who've become disenchanted with the established forces of law and order. They no longer trust them. Been victimised once too often. Needlessly stopped and searched. Gratuitous traffic violations. Day by day the rift is growing. The breakdown of trust. Many of us are now fearful of the very people we are paying to protect us.

MARTIN. Well, I think those are people with something to hide, that's all.

HILDA. Guilty consciences.

MARTIN. Exactly.

HILDA. I trust the police. Implicitly.

ROD. Just wait till it happens to you, Hilda …

HILDA. What?

ROD. *(darkly)* You'll see.

MAGDA. *(rising suddenly, urgently)* Sssh!

> *(The others look at her as* **MAGDA** *stares towards the window.)*

DOROTHY. What is it, dear?

MAGDA. I saw somebody out there in the field. I thought I did.

> *(***ROD** *moves swiftly to the window and, cupping his hands to the glass, strains to see out into the darkness.)*

MARTIN. Anything, Rod?

ROD. No. Nothing. Can't see anything. You did well to stay alert, though.

MARTIN. I have taken certain precautions, out there, since our incident. I've put up properly worded signs. Private property. Trespassers will be prosecuted. That sort of thing. At regular intervals along our boundary.

HILDA. Mind you, Martin, when it's dark they won't be able to read them.

ROD. I'll be amazed if half of them can read anyway.

MARTIN. Well, it's a gesture. It's a start. I take your point, Rod. We do need to take action certainly, but I believe it must fall well short of unprovoked violence.

HILDA. Hear, hear!

MARTIN. And I would at present prefer to maintain my trust in our police force. We can't proceed any further, at least until we've had a more formal meeting and hopefully had an official visit from a police representative

ROD. *(shrugging, hopelessly)* Well …

HILDA. I feel the same as Martin. I support my brother.

DOROTHY. I suppose you're right.

MAGDA. Yes.

HILDA. Well, on that note, shall we all adjourn for tea? Kettle should be about boiling. In here or in the kitchen, everyone? There's so few of us.

DOROTHY. Oh, kitchen. Every time. Nothing like it, is there, a cuppa in the kitchen?

HILDA. Yes, after all, we're all friends … If you care to follow me, everyone.

(They all rise and start to move to the kitchen door. Before anyone can leave the room, there comes a sudden, ear-splitting crash of breaking glass as the window is shattered and a projectile lands in the middle of the carpet where a few seconds ago some of them had been standing. **MAGDA** *screams,* **DOROTHY** *and* **HILDA** *cry out in surprise. The men express alarm.)*

GARETH. *(simultaneously with the women)* Look out!

ROD. *(simultaneously)* Get down! Get down! Hit the floor! *(He takes his own advice and lies down)*

MARTIN. *(simultaneously)* Oh my goodness, what on earth –?

(A stunned silence.)

*(***MARTIN*** is the first to move.)*

ROD. *(rising, cautiously)* Careful! It might be a grenade.

*(***MARTIN*** continues to approach the missile.)*

Careful … carefully, now …

HILDA. Be careful, Martin.

DOROTHY. Might be a bomb.

GARETH. Looks like a rock. A brick.

MARTIN. *(bending to pick up the debris)* No, it's – it's … Hilda, it's Monty.

HILDA. *(her hands to her mouth)* Oh, no, Martin! Not Monty …

ROD. *(sotto)* Monty? Who the hell's Monty?

MARTIN. He's … lost his little head … Hilda!

*(***MARTIN*** holds up the two halves of the broken gnome.)*

HILDA. Oh, no, no.

(**MARTIN**, *suddenly resolute, puts the two broken pieces down on the table.*)

MARTIN. *(grimly)* If this is how they want it. This is war. War.

(He strides to the shattered window.)

(Shouting out into the night) Alright! If that's the way you want it. This is war. Do you hear me? *(Yelling)* WAR!

(He turns and marches back across the room, shouldering through the others.)

Excuse me.

(**MARTIN** *exits to the kitchen. The others remain grouped, a little surprised by the change that their host has undergone. They all look to* **HILDA** *who now has a new gleam of battle in her eye.*)

HILDA. Alright, everyone, you heard my brother. Tea first. Then war!

(**HILDA** *goes out to the kitchen.*)

(As the others follow her, music as the lights fade to:)

Scene Three

(The same. Two weeks later.)

(Daytime. The window has been repaired.)

(MARTIN *enters briskly from the kitchen.)*

(HILDA *enters simultaneously from the hall.)*

(A brief pause while **MARTIN** *takes a breath, preparing himself. He has gained a new sense of authority.* **HILDA** *watches him, waiting.)*

HILDA. You ready?

MARTIN. Alright. Show him in. *(As she goes)* Make sure the others have some tea or coffee while they're waiting.

HILDA. I'm going to.

(HILDA *goes off to the front door.)*

(MARTIN *finds a more commanding position in the room to receive his guest.)*

(LUTHER *enters. He stops as he sees* **MARTIN**. **HILDA** *hovers behind him.)*

LUTHER. You are mad, do you know that? You are seriously deranged. Insane. Certifiable. You are an unhinged, dangerous psychopathic lunatic. In a nutshell, you are barking.

HILDA. *(stiffly)* If you'll excuse me. *(She makes to leave)*

LUTHER. And her. She's as mad as a hatter away with the fairies as well.

(HILDA *goes out.)*

MARTIN. *(with dignity)* Perhaps you would elaborate on those unsubstantiated accusations. If you wouldn't mind, Mr Bradley?

LUTHER. What the hell are you doing? What are you playing at? You've turned a nice, peaceful, respectable neighbourhood into a prison camp.

MARTIN. I feel that's a trifle of an exaggeration.

LUTHER. I mean, look at it! *(Indicating the window)* Ten foot security fences with razor wire. We're practically surrounded –

MARTIN. I trust we will be by the end of today, if the fencing contractors keep to schedule …

LUTHER. You cannot be serious …

MARTIN. … otherwise, we shall have to invoke penalty clauses …

LUTHER. … you intend to surround this entire development with fences?

MARTIN. That was the general consent of the majority at the full meeting. We took a ballot. I believe yours was a spoiled paper, Mr Bradley. Scrawling 'mad bastards' on it rendered your vote invalid.

LUTHER. How are people meant to get in or out of the place?

MARTIN. Through the main gate. They will simply need to produce their official identification card in order to gain admission. Similarly, getting out, they need only show their card which has been issued to every registered inhabitant and their dependants over the age of three …

LUTHER. I'm relieved to hear you're stopping short of full body searches anyway.

MARTIN. That is still under consideration by the relevant sub-committee.

LUTHER. I don't believe it. *(Producing a laminated ID card from his pocket)* By identity cards I take it we're talking about these things, are we? Which I found stuffed through my letter box this morning?

MARTIN. You and Mrs Bradley will both have been issued with one. I'm pleased to see you're already carrying it, Mr Bradley. Sound practice to get used to.

LUTHER. What is this thing?

MARTIN. If you read the back it is an Official Bluebell Development Identity Card. An O.B.D.I.C., for short. Everyone living in Bluebell Hill should, by this morning, have their own O.B.D.I.C. They were all delivered by my sister personally by hand.

LUTHER. On whose authority?

MARTIN. The Bluebell Hill Residents' Committee or, to be more accurate, The Bluebell Hill Residents' Security Sub-committee. All officially set up and voted in by a two-thirds majority of the residents.

LUTHER. Yes, I see you've managed to unite every weirdo, every fascist thug on this development, haven't you?

MARTIN. You're entitled to your personal view of your fellow residents, Mr Bradley, distasteful as it is. The committee has no particular political affiliations ...

LUTHER. Louts on every street corner in quasi-military uniforms ...

MARTIN. Street wardens. Officially appointed ...

LUTHER. ... thugs armed with baseball clubs and dogs patrolling all night ...

MARTIN. Regular patrols, all for your own safety, Mr Bradley. So you can sleep peacefully in your bed at night ...

LUTHER. Oh, yes, talking of sleep, what the bloody hell's going on with the street lighting these past few days?

MARTIN. We felt – the Environment Sub-committee felt – that the level of street illumination provided by the council was far from adequate and it was voted unanimously to supplement it –

LUTHER. Supplement it! It's broad daylight out there at midnight – how's anyone meant to get any sleep?

MARTIN. This is only the start, Mr Bradley. That's just phase one. Protection from the danger outside. From beyond the fence. Tomorrow sees the start of phase two.

LUTHER. Phase two? There's a phase two, for God's sake?

MARTIN. Indeed there is. The danger within, Mr Bradley. Inside the Bluebell Hill Development itself. Equally urgently, our community needs protecting just as much from itself. The committee will shortly be introducing regulations and guidelines, some voluntary, some mandatory, to inject a modicum of self-discipline, some much needed muscle tone into this flabby, out-of-condition body we call society. *(Growing in rhetoric as he speaks)* What you don't seem to realise, Mr Bradley, is that the actions we are taking are in direct response to desperate cries from desperate people. I'm talking about the elderly, Mr Bradley. I'm talking about women and children. People terrified to go out on their own and leave their homes unattended – oh, not just at night – that's bad enough – but, recently in the middle of the day, as well. Go out without being harassed, molested, threatened or made to feel fearful for their own safety. Oh, yes, Mr Bradley, I hear you say, well, if they feel that way, there are official authorities, surely they should turn to them. They should turn to the police. If they can ever find one or, if they're able to telephone and they don't get a recorded voice telling them that their call is important and being dealt with as soon as possible. "Help me, I'm a pensioner who's bleeding to death in a telephone box." The only box in the street that hasn't been vandalised. I'm talking about those people, Mr Bradley, the ones who feel powerless, who believe that there is no one left to turn to. Well, I'm saying to them, yes, there is someone. Pensioners, you can walk safely in daylight on your own street without feeling threatened, without being subjected to nine foot high, obscene graffiti on every street corner! Parents, you can feel confident your children are free to go outside to play! Women, you can now walk without fear alone at night! There is someone here for you! Speaking out for you! Fighting your corner! And that man is here, standing in front of you today! Thank you and bless you all!

(**MARTIN** *drops his head, exhausted.* **LUTHER** *stares at him incredulously.*)

LUTHER. *(quietly)* You are. You're completely mad. God help us all.

(*He throws the ID card down and turns to leave.*)

MARTIN. *(as* **LUTHER** *goes)* I wouldn't leave that behind, if I were you. If you don't have your identity card, not even God will be able to help you, Mr Bradley!

(**LUTHER** *goes out. The front door slams loudly. At once* **HILDA** *appears in the kitchen doorway. She has evidently been listening.*)

HILDA. You did your speech.

MARTIN. Some of it.

HILDA. Sounded wonderful. Through the door.

MARTIN. It needs a little more work.

HILDA. See how it goes tonight at the big meeting. Can I let them in, now?

MARTIN. Yes, of course.

HILDA. *(turning off and calling)* Would you all care to come in now?

(**HILDA** *admits* **DOROTHY, ROD, GARETH** *and finally* **MAGDA** *who, looking round nervously, sits silently throughout the next.*)

MARTIN. *(as they settle)* Ah! Welcome, welcome. Sorry to keep you waiting, everyone. Is this all there is of us? We seem rather depleted, this evening.

ROD. The Wrigley brothers had to leave, sent their apologies. They were due back on patrol.

MARTIN. Ah yes, the Wrigley family. Yes, you were right about them, Rod. Useful people to have on our side.

GARETH. I'd hate to be on their other side.

ROD. Well, the Wrigley family, you know. Tragic what's happened to them. Years of persecution. Years. First it was the father, Lee. Perfectly innocent second hand car dealer. Then his sons, Dirk and Duggie. Nicer couple of panel beaters you won't meet anywhere.

HILDA. Who's been persecuting them?

ROD. The police. That's why they were reluctant to join us, initially. Soon as they knew we were, you know, independent, they were on our side like a shot.

DOROTHY. You can understand the police being suspicious, though. With all those tattoos.

ROD. Since when's it been illegal to have a tattoo?

HILDA. No, it's rather what they say. I mean, that one on the younger boy's chest I found really offensive …

GARETH. You mean, KNEEL FOR IT BITCH, that one?

DOROTHY. Yes, that's really offensive. To women it is.

ROD. That's Duggie. I'll remind him to keep his shirt on in the house in future.

DOROTHY. Don't let Cissy and Sindy see it. They'll take real offence. Ex-navy girls, aren't they?

ROD. Cissy is. Sindy's a judo instructor. Yes, well, those two. They've got an agenda of their own, those two. Lesbians, of course.

HILDA. *(coolly)* I'm sorry, but I don't see that their sexual inclinations have anything to do with it.

ROD. Quite a lot to do with it, actually …

MARTIN. Now, then, if the meeting can come to order. I must hurry this through, if I may. I think we're barely quorate but since it's only by way of our bi-weekly catch up, I think we can proceed. Ignoring formalities if we may, oh – where's Amy – do we know where she is, Gareth?

GARETH. *(tersely)* No idea.

MARTIN. Oh, dear.

HILDA. Again.

MARTIN. So. Skimming through the minutes. Anything arising from these? Oh, yes, item four. That's you, Gareth? How are you getting on?

GARETH. Well, I've been hard at it, they're nearly completed … I'm pleased to report.

DOROTHY. It's taken long enough.

GARETH. Well, you need a good finish. I didn't want it to look half done.

ROD. They'll need a finish. Out in all weathers …

GARETH. That's the top of course. The exposed part. Teak finish. Then I've got the metal legs to rust-proof. They'll need to be sunk deep. We'll need the holes digging for those first. Then I have to pour the concrete …

DOROTHY. Where are you going to dig these holes?

MARTIN. If you recall, on the main ornamental roundabout, Dorothy. Just on the way in …

DOROTHY. On the ornamental roundabout? Oh, that's a shame, isn't it …?

MARTIN. … so they'll be in full view, you remember? We decided that a couple of meetings ago …

DOROTHY. Have to transplant the daffodils, won't they? They're looking a picture at the moment …

HILDA. Needs must.

DOROTHY. I don't know why we need stocks, I'm sure …

GARETH. To make a public example. Of someone.

DOROTHY. We've never needed stocks before, have we? Never had them before.

GARETH. Last used officially in 1872 in Wales.

DOROTHY. Oh, well, Wales …

MARTIN. Anyway. We agreed that the stocks are intended more as a deterrent. Hence their proposed high visibility. Probably never be used. I hope not, anyway. Still, well done, Gareth. Can we expect those by the end of the week?

GARETH. Oh, yes. Easily. Final coat, that's all.

DOROTHY. *(grumbling)* Next thing we'll be building a gallows …

MARTIN. *(briskly)* Yes, splendid. Rod? Anything?

ROD. Pleased to announce that vandalism is down another fourteen per cent. And as for graffiti, well, apart from the garage door at number fifteen and we know who that was. That's internal and can be sharply dealt with. His father's agreed to do that.

DOROTHY. Teach him to spell 'pouf' while he's at it …

ROD. The perimeter fence, I am assured by LGB Security, will be completed by tomorrow. They'll then start construction of the permanent main gate. Supplementary street lighting is all but complete. Nothing else to report.

MARTIN. Thank you, Rod. Keep up the good work. Hilda?

HILDA. Yes. O.B.D.I.C's were all distributed this morning. Everyone I've seen so far seems happy enough with them. Apart from –

MARTIN. *(with a glance at **MAGDA**)* Oh, yes. Just pop it through his door again a bit later. When he's had time to reconsider …

HILDA. I will. I wanted to raise one issue regarding the main gate. Once that's in place and we have full security, I do think we should consider, Chairman, searches both on the way in and when leaving. Going out to discourage petty pilfering. Coming in, to stop the importing of – unsuitable items.

GARETH. Unsuitable items?

HILDA. I was thinking of weapons, drugs and alcohol.

ROD. Alcohol?

HILDA. In excess.

DOROTHY. Oh, I don't know. I'd miss my little tipple. I mean, mainly at Christmas but –

MARTIN. Well, we could consider it. There is already the street ban on public drinking. I don't think we can prevent it in people's own homes. Within moderation.

HILDA. Depends what you call moderation. There's one or two people living on the hill whose behaviour I would describe as far from moderate.

DOROTHY. I think we all know who that is ...

GARETH. *(rising, agitatedly)* Yes, we do. We do! We do!

MARTIN. Yes, as I say, we can certainly consider it ...

HILDA. The sooner the better, if you ask me ...

GARETH. *(as he leaves)* Excuse me, Chairman. Goodnight, everyone ...

MARTIN. *(continuing unperturbed)* ... sound out public feeling and.... Oh, goodnight, Gareth ... take the temperature of the water, as it were ...

*(**GARETH** goes out to the front door. **DOROTHY** rises.)*

MARTIN. *(contd.)* ... maybe we can relax things a little at Christmas time ...

DOROTHY. *(sotto)* Excuse me, please, Chairman, I have to ...

*(**DOROTHY** tugs **MAGDA**'s sleeve and indicates that she should follow her.)*

MARTIN. ... that might be a sensible compromise, mightn't it? That might be a sensible way round it ... goodnight, Dorothy ... goodnight, Magda ...

MAGDA. *(sotto)* Goodnight ...

*(**DOROTHY** and **MAGDA** creep to the front door.)*

MARTIN. *(conscious that he has lost the attention of the meeting)* ... yes, we'll need to minute that. To be discussed in full committee. Well, in the absence of Amy, Mrs Janner, in that case, I think I can declare –

HILDA. I don't know why you stand up for her, Martin, I really don't.

MARTIN. Now, Hilda, this is neither the time nor place to –

*(**ROD** rises.)*

HILDA. She's continually late. She's rude. Wandering the streets with glasses of alcohol, in front of young children …

ROD. *(sotto)* Excuse me, Chairman. Need to get on …

*(**ROD** creeps to the front door.)*

HILDA. … blatantly carrying on her – dalliances. Nobody says a word to her. That poor man, her husband. Day after day, he sits on this committee, whenever she's brought up you sweep it under the carpet. If we need to make an example of anybody, we should start with her.

MARTIN. Now, now, really. I must, as chairman, declare that out of order, Hilda.

HILDA. She's the devil, Martin. She's a child of the devil.

MARTIN. If you wish to register a formal complaint against Amy – against Mrs Janner – you know the rules as well as I do. You must do so in writing, within ten days, to the Morality Sub-committee. In the meantime, I'm not prepared to discuss it with you, Hilda.

HILDA. What's happening to you, Martin? One minute you're so inspiring, such a source of – radiance … and then … What's got into you?

MARTIN. To be honest, I'm not entirely sure myself, Hilda.

*(The front doorbell rings. **HILDA** looks at him. Then she rises and goes out to the front door.)*

*(**MARTIN** shuffles his papers.)*

*(**HILDA** returns with **AMY**.)*

AMY. *(as she enters)* Whew! Nice and warm in here. Freezing out.

*(**AMY** throws herself on the sofa, pulling off her silk scarf as she does so)* Have I missed anything vital?

MARTIN. *(looking at HILDA, awkwardly)* – er …

AMY. Yes? No? What's been happening? *(She smiles at **HILDA**)*

HILDA. I think the chairman would like a private word with you, Mrs Janner. Excuse me.

(**HILDA** *leaves.*)

(*A silence.*)

AMY. *(laughing)* God! I feel I'm back in the head-teacher's study. Help! What have I done? Late again, Mrs Janner. This really will not do.

(*She rises and goes to the window.* **MARTIN** *watches her uncomfortably.*)

God, that fence is enormous. Don't you mind it? Oh, just look, Jesus has come out of his bushes! I bet he's happy about that. He's taken Monty's place. Sorry, the late Monty. Sorry, Martin, I know you were fond of Monty. Poor Montmorency.

(*A silence.*)

If you don't say something to me soon, Martin, I'm going home. The silence is killing me. I mean, what? Ten minutes late? Twenty? Come on …

MARTIN. It's not just lateness, Amy. There've been concerns expressed.

AMY. Concerns? What concerns?

MARTIN. From the committee. About your general behaviour.

AMY. Oh, my God. I am up before the headmaster. What am I going to get? Six of the best, sir?

MARTIN. Now, don't be frivolous, Amy. This is no laughing matter. There are certain people on the committee who feel – you should no longer serve on it. I'm not one of them, but …

AMY. Oh, Christ! Honestly! *(With a wave to the garden)* Sorry, Jesus, but Christ, Martin! Just look who's on that fucking committee, will you …?

MARTIN. Please, Amy! Please!

AMY. Sorry, swearing. Mustn't swear, not in here. Naughty girl. Sorry! Just look who's on it. My husband for one. My sad, inadequate husband who can't even bear to be in the house with me. Sitting in his – effing shed, wanking, and leaving me on my effing own for days on end so in the end I'm forced – in effing desperation – to find – someone else ... only to find his own sad, effing little child bride is also on the committee!

MARTIN. Yes, I know all this, Amy. Everyone knows. But just why you need to make it all so public, I don't understand. *(Growing very upset)* I don't know why you insist on behaving like this. You're a beautiful woman, Amy. You – demean yourself – I can't bear to see it. You and that Luther man next door. He's a bully and he's an idiot ...

AMY. True. He is.

MARTIN. And we suspect he beats his wife.

AMY. Probably. Luther can be quite brutal occasionally ...

MARTIN. Has he – with you?

AMY. Nothing I can't handle, darling. Don't worry, I give as good as I get.

MARTIN. You know I'm very fond of you, Amy. I ...

AMY. Well, let's not go there. Otherwise we'll have big sister after us, won't we?

MARTIN. Hilda? ... Hilda won't ...

AMY. She loathes me. Come on. She does. All because I accidentally insulted her fucking awful green wallpaper. Complete with her sickly green paintwork ... Sorry, I'm swearing again.

(MARTIN sits miserably. AMY, during the next, gradually moves closer to him.)

AMY. *(contd.)* Cheer up, Martin. You must know why I'm behaving so badly. Surely you know why. I'm like a child who hasn't got what she wants. The man she wants. Because he doesn't want her. Vicious circle, really. The more she wants him and can't have him, the worse she behaves. And the worse she behaves, the less he wants her. There's no solution, is there? It's an unbreakable vicious circle, really. Unless the man she wants so badly was suddenly to put her out of her misery. Please, Martin. Save me. Will you save me, please?

(She is now standing over him. MARTIN stands to face her. They are now very close. After a second, MARTIN yields to temptation and kisses her for a brief second gently on the lips as if tasting forbidden fruit. They look at each other. He evidently enjoys his first taste for he repeats the experiment, kissing her again. He leans forward for a third tasting but AMY responds this time, taking his head in her hands and kissing him deeply and passionately. It is a long kiss. Too much for MARTIN who is hyperventilating slightly as they break. He sits back rather dizzily.)

AMY. *(gently)* Thank you. Goodnight, my darling.

(AMY goes out, leaving her scarf.)

(MARTIN sits for a moment, rather dazed.)

(The front door closes.)

MARTIN. *(dazed)* Oh, dear God. Dear God.

(HILDA enters from the kitchen, watching him.)

(MARTIN finally becomes aware of her.)

You're right, Hilda. She is the devil and I'm probably going to hell. But, God forgive me, I'm going to enjoy it.

(MARTIN goes out to the hall. HILDA watches him go. She is about to return to the kitchen when she sees AMY's bright silk scarf (probably red!) lying on the sofa. HILDA gathers it up. There is a gleam of battle in her eye. She rips the scarf in half.)

HILDA. *(closing her eyes, in prayer)* Dear Lord, help me to save my brother! Help me to save him!

(As HILDA turns to go off, the lights fade to a blackout.)

End of ACT I

Act II

Scene One

(The same.)

(A day or two later. The committee, **MARTIN**, **HILDA**, **DOROTHY**, **GARETH** *and* **ROD**, *are midway through a meeting.)*

MARTIN. … so, what's next, marketing and press? Dorothy, I think that's now your area of responsibility, isn't it? And may I comment from the chair and say how well you're handling things.

HILDA. Hear! Hear!

DOROTHY. *(modestly)* … as I say I have had brief experience. It was a while ago, mind you. Fifteen years on the *Advertiser*.

GARETH. As a reporter?

DOROTHY. No, I was in charge of small ads, mainly. But I did get a good understanding of the way a journalist's mind works …

MARTIN. Yes, as I say, you're doing a wonderful job, Dorothy, keep it up.

GARETH. Did you see the headline in the *Daily Mail* this morning? Front page.

ROD. Couldn't miss it, could you?

GARETH. How did it go? "Is this the man to run the country?"

DOROTHY. <u>Our</u> country. To run <u>our</u> country.

MARTIN. *(modestly)* Well … who reads the *Mail*?

GARETH. Almost everyone round here.

DOROTHY. Except for him next door, Bradley. *Guardian* reader, isn't he?

ROD. No wonder he's misguided.

HILDA. Lovely big picture of Martin, too. Glad you wore that pullover.

MARTIN. You were right, Hilda. Set it off just right.

DOROTHY. Sitting next to the pillory.

GARETH. No, I have to correct you there, Dorothy. They're stocks, not a pillory. I keep saying …

DOROTHY. That's what they called it in the article.

GARETH. *(on his specialist subject)* Yes, well they got it wrong. It's a common enough mistake. Stocks and pillory. People often get them muddled. With stocks, like we have, you're sat down with your feet secured, you see. Whereas with a pillory, you're standing, you see, with your head and arms trapped – like this, you see – more painful – much more vulnerable – generally, the pillory used to be for more drastic offences. Excruciating. I'd be happy to build one of those as well, if you—

MARTIN. No, I think we're happy enough with the stocks at the moment, Gareth. Thank you for the offer. I think the stocks, displayed in that prominent position on the miniature roundabout, are having a beneficial effect, certainly as regards petty offences, anyway. Wouldn't you say so, Rod?

ROD. As far as we can tell. Anti-social behaviour and petty theft all down another five per cent. Vandalism practically zero last month. Would have been but for Mrs Bale losing control of her mobility scooter and damaging Mr Choker's bay tree …

HILDA. You can hardly call that vandalism, can you?

ROD. Derek Choker did. That's not all he called her.

DOROTHY. Accidents happen. They're very difficult to control those things, especially for the disabled …

MARTIN. Yes, well, moving on …

GARETH. Could I – through the chair if I may – put in a final word on the stocks …?

MARTIN. Sorry?

GARETH. The stocks, the ones I took time and trouble building. I'd like to say, I'm dismayed, not to say disappointed, at their lack of use. They appear, in my view, to be underused. In the end, it's not for me to say how or when they should be used. That's down to the D and P sub-committee. But I did spend a time-consuming number of man hours building those without, I remind you, without a penny of remuneration towards labour costs—

ROD. D and P did provide materials, Gareth …

GARETH. Yes, all the same. I had hoped the stocks would have been used more – that's all I'm saying. I'm very disappointed …

HILDA. You can hardly say they haven't been used.

ROD. *(consulting his notes)* They've been used so far on fifteen separate occasions. Mostly juveniles. Failing to observe the underage curfew. Illegal consumption of alcohol. Causing an affray. Foul language in a public place … that's the most common. Mind you, while we're on the topic, Gareth, when you've a minute to spare, you might consider reducing the size of those foot apertures. Some of these anorexic teenage girls they just slip out of them, walk away laughing, calm as you like. Makes a mockery of justice.

GARETH. *(huffily)* I didn't design them for teenage girls, Rod. I designed them for – maturer wom— people. People like – I mean, if they're never used on the people they were intended to be used on … On those they rightly ought to be used on … I mean, what's the point in my – ? What's the point? What's the …? *(Tearfully)* I don't see the point …?

(The others are very embarrassed.)

MARTIN. *(calming him)* Yes, alright, Gareth. Point taken. I mean, as you correctly say, use of the stocks is really down to D and P. The Discipline and Punishment Sub-committee must, in the end, be the sole arbiter. Otherwise there's anarchy. We'd all of us be punishing just who we felt like, wouldn't we? No, the law, even our law, must remain above personal feelings. Right. So. Proceeding on. Oh, we're on item seven. That's you, isn't it, Gareth? Anything to report?

GARETH. *(muttering tearfully)* I'm working on various – types – of devices …

MARTIN. *(having trouble hearing)* I'm sorry, what? Types of what?

GARETH. *(still barely audible)* … devices … manacles… metal collars … leg irons and other forms of restraint … but … but …

(The others have all been forced to lean in to hear what **GARETH** *is saying.)*

HILDA. I'm sorry, Gareth. None of us can hear you, love. You must speak up.

*(***GARETH*** springs to his feet and runs to the front door.)*

GARETH. *(distraught, loudly)* What's the point? What's the point? She's never coming back, now! Never!

*(***GARETH*** exits.)*

(A brief silence. The others are rather stunned by this unaccustomed outburst.)

ROD. *(finally)* He's becoming a liability, that bloke. He's obsessed with that wife of his. He's right. He'll never get her back. Never. She doesn't want him. She's not worth it. He should have shown her the door ages ago.

MARTIN. Yes, he should.

ROD. That's what I did with my wife. Eight years with me. Don't like it under my roof? Out you go! Out she went.

DOROTHY. They've stopped seeing each other, anyway. Her and – him next door, that Bradley man. Haven't been near each other for days.

ROD. You're sure of that?

DOROTHY. I'm right opposite. Della's next door but one. She's seen nothing. And she sees everything. I must say it's a relief Amy's no longer on this committee. When I heard she'd resigned, I breathed a sigh of relief …

ROD. As did we all.

DOROTHY. I think that quiet word you had with her the other day, Martin, had an effect. Don't you think?

HILDA. Oh, yes.

ROD. Certainly.

DOROTHY. Well done. Whatever you said to her – I think Mrs Janner seems to have reformed her ways. And for that I think we must thank our chairman. I think that ought to be minuted, don't you, everybody?

ROD. Unless they're going elsewhere for it.

DOROTHY. Somewhere else?

ROD. Away from Bluebell Hill. Meeting up somewhere else, her and Bradley. Having it away somewhere in another part of town.

DOROTHY. Where? Where would they go?

ROD. I don't know. His office?

DOROTHY. He's a dry cleaner, isn't he?

ROD. A hotel, then? It's easy enough to verify anyway. I'll check the main gate log. The O.B.D.I.C. register. If they're both sneaking off in secret, their movements ought to coincide.

MARTIN. What they get up to off this development isn't strictly our concern though, is it?

HILDA. Be interesting to see, though.

MARTIN. No, no. We must assume, as far as Amy, Mrs Janner, is concerned, that matter is now closed.

DOROTHY. Still won't help Gareth, will it, poor man? If she still isn't coming home to him. I don't know why she stays married to him.

HILDA. I wonder.

MARTIN. Well, we can but conjecture. Who knows what goes on in a woman's mind, eh, Rod?

(ROD shakes his head.)

MARTIN. (*contd.*) Right, item eight. Luther Bradley. What's the latest there?

ROD. Well, as you know, he's been going round The Hill, door to door, trying to canvass support. Mustering opposition to the Committee where he can, if he can …

DOROTHY. Is he having any luck so far?

ROD. People are generally standing solid behind us. One or two waiverers. Like that dodgy pair at number fifteen.

HILDA. They're nothing much to worry about.

DOROTHY. They're thinking of splitting up, anyway, so I've heard. Since Gavin had a fling with one of the fencing men. Micky was in floods of tears for days.

HILDA. What are we going to do about Bradley? Before he gains support.

ROD. I could ask the Wrigleys to pop in on him, have a quiet word.

MARTIN. Oh, no, I don't think that's wise …

HILDA. That would probably turn him into a martyr, by the time the Wrigleys had finished. We know them and their quiet words.

DOROTHY. Mrs Trace-Wallace's poodle …

HILDA. Quite.

ROD. Now, we have no evidence of their involvement. You can't lay that at the Wrigleys' door, no way …

DOROTHY. No, it was laid at her door, wasn't it? Poor little thing …

MARTIN. No, Hilda's right. Any threats towards Bradley will put the whole of Bluebell Hill on his side …

DOROTHY. Including the press. They're on our side at the moment. I've got lots of follow up requests after that *Daily Mail* piece. They'll all want to talk to you, Martin.

MARTIN. Oh dear. Why me?

HILDA. Because you're our leader, Martin. Our inspiration. Our guiding light.

ROD. Martin's also the prime target.

MARTIN. Prime target? How do you mean?

ROD. For Luther Bradley. If he can bring you down, he'll reckon he's half-way to winning.

DOROTHY. He'll never bring Martin down. Like to see him try, eh, Hilda?

HILDA. *(less sure)* Yes.

ROD. Unless he rakes up all that business with Dudgeon. And the lad with the clarinet.

HILDA. I thought that had all gone away.

ROD. He'll try and bring it back again. Molesting a child musical prodigy never goes away, especially if the gutter press get hold of it...

MARTIN. It was a genuine misunderstanding, that's all it was. There's no story there, surely?

DOROTHY. Show me a good man, I'll show you a smear campaign ... I know that from the *Advertiser*. We brought one labour councillor to his knees.

HILDA. We have to nip that in the bud, don't we?

MARTIN. A misunderstanding between me and the lad's father, Mr Dudgeon.

ROD. Yes, well, you can trust him about as far as you can kick a lead football. If he can make a few quid out of it, he will. Amazed he hasn't already.

DOROTHY. Perhaps he's not a *Daily Mail* reader?

ROD. Bit above his head.

HILDA. Maybe Mr Dudgeon is worth a visit from the Wrigleys, do you think?

ROD. Right. Like with like.

HILDA. Nothing heavy-handed, mind you. Just to remind Mr Dudgeon that the whole incident is behind us. Just to remind him in case he'd forgotten that he promised he wasn't going to remember.

DOROTHY. What do you think, Martin?

MARTIN. *(doubtfully)* Yes. Possibly. If you really think the Wrigleys can be relied upon to – tread carefully.

ROD. Oh, yes. I'll tell them you said to tread carefully. They'll do that for you, Martin, they respect you. You're some sort of hero to them now.

MARTIN. Really? That's nice to hear.

ROD. Particularly the two lads, Dirk and Duggie.

MARTIN. And – the youngest one – Duggie, is it? He's – calmer these days, is he?

ROD. Oh, yes. Since he's been on the medication, he's back to normal. Well, as normal as Duggie can get, you know …

MARTIN. Only we don't want gratuitous violence, that's not in our creed, Rod.

HILDA. No part of our creed.

DOROTHY. Certainly not.

ROD. I'll arrange for them to take a trip down to the Mountjoy, then. Visit Barry Dudgeon.

HILDA. The sooner the better.

ROD. *(rising)* I'll make the call. If you'll excuse me, Chairman.

MARTIN. Of course.

(**ROD** *goes out to the hall to make his call.*)

That deals with Mr Dudgeon, I think …

DOROTHY. How are we going to deal with Luther Bradley?

HILDA. Where's he most vulnerable? We can forget his extra-marital goings on, they're all in the past, according to Dorothy.

DOROTHY. I'm certain they are.

HILDA. So, what else is there? No misdemeanours, has he?

DOROTHY. Nothing to hit the headlines.

HILDA. We need something big, something emotive that'll catch the public imagination, as I think you're wont to say in your line, Dorothy.

DOROTHY. *(tentatively)* Well, of course, there's always his wife. There's Magda.

HILDA. Brilliant, Dorothy, why didn't I think of that? Of course! Magda! You're brilliant!

DOROTHY. *(modestly)* I just remembered, that's all …

MARTIN. Listen, don't you thinks this all smacks a little bit of blackmail? A bit immoral, isn't it?

HILDA. What, bringing a wife beater to justice? What's immoral about that?

MARTIN. Yes, but we're using it for … *(He shrugs and gives up)*

HILDA. We'd need to persuade Magda to testify. Against her husband.

DOROTHY. Well. They're either eager to pour it all out to someone, or else they clam up completely, they're trying to protect the bloke … I think Magda might be that sort.

HILDA. We could talk to her. Have a quiet word. Informally.

DOROTHY. You're close to her, Hilda. It would need to be a woman.

MARTIN. Anyone but the Wrigley brothers.

HILDA. Well, I don't mind. I think Magda trusts me.

DOROTHY. Oh yes, she does. She seems very fond of you.

MARTIN. Well, shall we arrange that? Have a word with her at some stage soon.

HILDA. No time like the present, is there? I'll give her a call, then.

MARTIN. What, this minute?

HILDA. *(rather awkwardly)* I – had a feeling this might be an option. I had a word with Magda earlier. She's awaiting my call …

*(**HILDA** starts dialling her mobile.)*

DOROTHY. Oh, Hilda, you're so crafty. You planned this, didn't you? All along? *(To **MARTIN**)* Isn't she the crafty one?

MARTIN. *(looking at* **HILDA** *a little anxiously)* Yes – she can be. Pretty crafty.

(**DOROTHY** *has started studying her own mobile phone.*)

(**ROD** *sticks his head round the door.*)

HILDA. *(into her phone, under the next)* Hallo, Magda … it's Hilda from next door… yes … if you could … nothing serious, dear … nothing to worry about. Yes. We're just next door. See you in a minute. *(She rings off)*

DOROTHY. *(examining her phone, simultaneously)* Oh, look at all these! There's dozens more messages. What have we started?

ROD. *(over this)* That's all in hand, Martin. The Wrigleys. They're on their way down there.

MARTIN. Oh, good. Gently, remember, gently.

ROD. Oh, yes. Gently. The meeting's winding up, is it?

MARTIN. *(taking in the activity)* It appears to be, yes.

HILDA. *(ending her call)* Magda's coming straight round.

DOROTHY. *(still examining her phone)* Dozens of messages … they all want to talk to us, now. Wanting a word with our future Prime Minister probably.

MARTIN. One step at a time, Dorothy, one step at a time.

ROD. *(as he goes out again)* I'll be in touch, Martin …

MARTIN. Cheers, Rod. I'll see you out. I'll let her in when she arrives, Hilda. I'll be in the study.

(**MARTIN** *and* **ROD** *go out to the front door.*)

DOROTHY. Oh. You've got a study now?

HILDA. Just the dining room table with a cover over it.

DOROTHY. He needs a study. Now he's a leader. He needs a study. You know, I think that might be a photo opportunity.

HILDA. Martin needs – protecting over the next few weeks, Dorothy. We need to take care of him, all of us.

DOROTHY. His image, you mean?

HILDA. You were right. Show me a good man, I'll show you a smear campaign.

DOROTHY. They'll be lying in wait for him. That's the way their minds work.

HILDA. Prowling, like the troops of Midian ...

DOROTHY. Beg your pardon?

HILDA. Martin's our beacon, Dorothy, our shining light. We mustn't allow that light to be dimmed by the forces of darkness ...

DOROTHY. Well, no. I've heard the press called a lot of things but that's a new one.

HILDA. It's not just the press I'm talking about ...

DOROTHY. *(intrigued)* Oh, who else?

(The doorbell rings.)

HILDA. That's her. Dorothy, I wonder would you mind staying a minute or two longer. I think it'd be better with the two of us ...

DOROTHY. Are you sure? You don't think she'd be more relaxed, one to one?

HILDA. No, it's just if she does say anything I'd prefer it if there was a witness.

DOROTHY. Oh, you're crafty. Machiavellian, aren't you?

*(**MAGDA** enters tentatively from the hall. She hangs back in the doorway when she sees them.)*

MAGDA. Hallo ...

HILDA. Hallo, Magda.

DOROTHY. Hallo, dear ...

HILDA. Come in. Come and sit down. It's just us.

MAGDA. *(nervously smiling)* Thank goodness for that. I thought I was going to have to appear before the whole committee ...

HILDA. Oh, no, no...

DOROTHY. No.

MAGDA. ... I wondered what I could have done wrong ...

HILDA. Sit down. Sit down here by me.

(**HILDA** *places* **MAGDA** *between herself and* **DOROTHY**, *causing* **MAGDA** *to turn awkwardly this way and that throughout the scene.*)

(*addressing her rather like she would a child*) So. What have you been up to this morning, Magda?

MAGDA. (*guiltily*) How do you mean?

HILDA. Been doing anything interesting?

MAGDA. Oh, I see. Just my regular practice. You know.

DOROTHY. On your clarinet?

MAGDA. Yes – no, oboe. Mozart. The oboe quartet.

HILDA. Oh. You play the oboe as well?

MAGDA. Yes. Clarinet and oboe. Cor anglais occasionally.

DOROTHY. You're multi-talented, then?

MAGDA. Not really. Clarinet's my main instrument but I try to keep up my practice with the others.

HILDA. Flute?

MAGDA. Sorry?

HILDA. Flute? Do you play the flute as well?

MAGDA. Oh, no. Not flute. That's different … Just those three. Clarinet. And oboe and cor anglais. The cor anglais is quite similar to the oboe, actually. It's just a fifth lower … in tone, you know. It's bigger. Slightly longer.

DOROTHY. More difficult to carry around, then?

MAGDA. (*slightly confused*) Sorry?

HILDA. (*briskly interceding*) You're feeling alright now, then, Magda? Alright in yourself?

MAGDA. Yes, of course. Fine.

HILDA. Only I heard on the grapevine, Magda, that you fainted in the street the other day. Is that right?

DOROTHY. (*this is news to her*) Did you?

MAGDA. Well, I … no … no … I felt a bit dizzy, that's all, faint, you know. I didn't exactly faint. Not faint exactly …

HILDA. Well, what's in a word? Probably this muggy weather. Enough to make anyone faint, isn't it? I got very worried for you, when I heard.

MAGDA. Thank you. There was no need, as I say … Everyone was very helpful.

HILDA. They helped you home safely, then?

MAGDA. Yes.

HILDA. Got you to put your feet up?

MAGDA. Yes.

HILDA. This'll be Cissy and Sindy from number sixteen?

MAGDA. Yes, they were specially helpful. As I say, there was no need. I was perfectly … I mean, I was fine.

HILDA. Sindy tells me that while they were helping you to – relax, while they were helping you to loosen your clothing, they couldn't help noticing the bruises.

MAGDA. Bruises?

HILDA. Quite nasty bruises, Magda. On your arms. And – your upper torso.

MAGDA. Yes, well, I can be very clumsy … always bumping into … things, you know …

HILDA. There were also bruises on your back, Magda.

MAGDA. Really, well, I can't explain how on earth they—

HILDA. As well as – lower back. Bruises. Consistent with someone using a rod or a cane … Can you explain those, then?

MAGDA. That's ridiculous. They're making it up. Nonsense! They had no right to say that! Telling everyone. It's all rubbish. Absolute rubbish!

HILDA. So if we were to ask you to slip off your sweater and show us your arms and your back –

MAGDA. Certainly not! I'm not stripping off, what are you talking about?

HILDA. There's only us women here, Magda.

MAGDA. *(very flustered)* Listen. I'm sorry, I'm leaving. I'm not – This is ridiculous. They're lying. I'm going home.

HILDA. *(calmly)* Alright, if you'd prefer not to tell us, Magda, that's quite alright. We didn't mean to upset you, love. Off you go.

MAGDA. *(rising)* It's ridiculous. Ridiculous! I mean … honestly!

HILDA. Off you go. We won't say another word about it, I promise.

(**MAGDA** *moves to the door. But halfway there, her resolution wavers. She hesitates as if torn between speaking and maintaining her silence.*)

(*The others watch her, waiting.*)

(**MAGDA** *is silent for a moment.*)

MAGDA. *(without looking at them)* He promised. He promised Daddy, you see. Daddy made him promise. To – look after me. I was special. Daddy said I was special. After Mummy – after she – went away. He told me I was even more special. And I had to try harder than ever. To do everything extra well. He used to make me practise, do my lessons. Every day. Watching over me. If I was good, well done Magda, clever girl. And other times he'd – if I wasn't good – when I was bad he'd smack me – only to make me better, that's all – and later – when I was really bad, when I became really wicked, then he would really … you know. And then Daddy got ill and he was – he wasn't able to … Then there was Luther, you see. "Luther, look after my little girl." That's what he'd say. "I'm trusting you, Luther, when I'm not here to take care of her. She's the best daughter in the world but there's times when she can be so wicked. There's wickedness in her. We must help her, she needs our help." So then… after … then Luther … But they're liars, you see, those women who told you. They're wicked people, too. Just as wicked. Loving each other. Daddy said that was very, very wrong. That was evil. People like that were evil. And I was never to feel like that ever. <u>Ever</u>. Or else I would burn in hell forever. For ever … *(She hesitates)*

HILDA. *(gently)* Do you still feel like that, Magda? Do you still have those feelings inside you?

MAGDA. Sometimes. Some days. They won't go away, you see. No matter how hard I try. I do try. I promise I do. But some days the evil just grows and grows inside, no matter how hard I try to … And then I ask Luther – to help to stop them. I have to ask him to stop them.

(A slight pause.)

*(**DOROTHY** is crying quietly.)*

*(**HILDA**, for once, is lost for words.)*

I'm sorry, I must go home now to practise. The music is good. The music helps … Excuse me.

*(**MAGDA** goes out towards the front door.)*

HILDA. *(softly)* Dear God …

DOROTHY. *(dabbing her eyes)* What terrible things we do to children sometimes, don't we?

HILDA. God forgive him. All in the name of love. We do terrible things to that, as well. The name of love.

(Slight pause.)

Well. She's hardly going to testify against him, is she? The state she's in.

DOROTHY. But he beats her. He can't deny that …

HILDA. Oh, no. He won't deny it, but if she doesn't object, he'll claim they're private acts between consenting adults … When you think what he could have done for her. Taken her to see someone, straightened her out. All that music muddying her head. I never cared for Mozart, you know. I think he's greatly over-rated. I prefer Percy Grainger …

*(**MAGDA** comes hurriedly back from the hall.)*

MAGDA. *(as she enters, in panic)* He's coming! He's coming up the drive.

HILDA. Who is?

MAGDA. Luther. He saw me coming out. He'd told me never to come here again!

HILDA. Did you close the front door?

LUTHER. *(off, yelling)* Magda!

HILDA. Apparently not.

LUTHER. *(off)* MAGDA!

(**MAGDA** *scurries into a far corner of the room furthest from the hall doorway.*)

(**LUTHER** *enters, incandescent with rage.*)

(*Simultaneously, from the kitchen doorway,* **MARTIN** *enters in response to the disturbance.*)

LUTHER. *(as he enters)* Magda!

MAGDA. *(terrified)* Please! I didn't ... I didn't ...

(**LUTHER** *starts to advance on* **MAGDA**.)

LUTHER. What did I tell you? Didn't I tell you never to come here again?

HILDA. You stay away from her, please!

DOROTHY. Stay away!

LUTHER. *(loudly)* Keep out of it! This is a private personal matter between me and my wife.

(**MARTIN** *steps forward, so he is in direct line between* **LUTHER** *and* **MAGDA**, *blocking* **LUTHER**'s *path.*)

MARTIN. *(as he does this)* Oh, no, it's not. This is between you and me, Mr Bradley.

LUTHER. Get out of my bloody way! I've said this is a—

MARTIN. It may be a private personal matter but considering the volume at which you are conducting it, Mr Bradley, I think we can hardly term it personal, and certainly not private.

LUTHER. Stand aside.

MARTIN. I'm sorry. No. My house. My rules.

LUTHER. If you don't step aside, I'm going to have to make you.

MARTIN. Please leave immediately.

LUTHER. I'm warning you – I'll hit you.

MARTIN. *(removing his glasses)* Then you'll have to do that, won't you, Mr Bradley?

HILDA. *(softly, fearful for him)* Martin …!

(LUTHER punches MARTIN on the side of the face.)

(HILDA gasps. DOROTHY gives a little scream, MAGDA a little squeak of fear.)

(MARTIN staggers but retains his balance and remains facing LUTHER.)

LUTHER. Now will you get out of my way?

(MARTIN is evidently in some pain and, we suspect, barely able to focus.)

MARTIN. *(swaying slightly, shakily)* Alright. You've made your point, Mr Bradley. I hope that makes you feel better. Now leave my house at once, please.

LUTHER. I'll hit you again, I warn you.

MARTIN. You're perfectly at liberty to do that, Mr Bradley. Nobody here can stop you, least of all me. I should warn you, though, that I am a practising pacifist and I will not make any attempt to hit you back in return. In which case, you will have to continue hitting a defenceless man until he finally falls down at your feet in front of three witnesses and have that on your conscience for the rest of your life.

(LUTHER seems a little confused by this. MARTIN braces himself for a second blow.)

(LUTHER considers whether or not to hit MARTIN again.)

(The others wait with baited breath.)

(In the end **LUTHER** *decides against further action. He moves back to the doorway.)*

MARTIN. *(contd., replacing his glasses)* Thank you. Close the front door on your way out, please.

LUTHER. *(pausing briefly)* You have not heard the end of this. *(As he goes out)* No way! *(Off, from the hall)* NO WAY!

(The front door, off, slams violently.)

*(***MARTIN*** relaxes and staggers.)*

MARTIN. *(his head swimming)* Oh! Oh! Oh! Oh!

*(***MAGDA*** rushes to him and embraces him, nearly knocking him over.)*

MAGDA. *(in tearful relief)* Oh! *(As she hugs* **MARTIN***)* Oh! Oh! Oh! Oh!

MARTIN. Oh!

HILDA. Oh, Martin. Oh, I'm so proud of you!

DOROTHY. *(half to herself)* Oh, our future Prime Minister! Oh! Oh! Oh!

MARTIN. *(now distinctly groggy)* That saw him off, anyway. Saw him off. *(As* **MAGDA** *continues to cling to him)* Excuse me, Magda, would you mind not squeezing quite so tightly, dear?

HILDA. *(prising* **MAGDA** *off him, taking charge)* That's it, Magda. That'll do! Martin, sit down before you fall down. Dorothy!

DOROTHY. Yes?

HILDA. See where Luther's gone. Is he waiting outside there? Have a look!

*(***DOROTHY*** hurries off to the hall momentarily.)*

(To **MAGDA***)* You're certainly not going home again. The man's obviously completely out of control. You're stopping here …

MAGDA. But there's all my … I can't …

HILDA. We'll fetch your things over, don't worry. That'll be alright, won't it, Martin?

MARTIN. *(groggily)* What's that?

HILDA. If Magda has the spare room? Just for a day or two …?

MARTIN. *(only half with it)* Oh, yes …

HILDA. We're not expecting Auntie Joan till next month …

*(**DOROTHY** returns from the hall.)*

Is he still there?

DOROTHY. No, he's walking off down the road. Talking to himself it looks like …

HILDA. In which direction?

DOROTHY. Towards the main gate. Looks like he's going into town …

HILDA. Right. In that case, go next door with Magda and collect up as much of her stuff as she needs. And bring her back here. You show Dorothy what you want to bring, Magda. Some of your clothes and your – oboes and so on. You understand?

MAGDA. *(meekly)* Yes.

DOROTHY. *(taking **MAGDA**'s arm)* Come on, then, dear. Before he comes back.

*(**DOROTHY** hustles **MAGDA** towards the front door.)*

*(**HILDA** returns to minister to **MARTIN**. She tilts his head towards the light.)*

HILDA. Oh, yes, you'll have a nasty bruise. I'll get some ice. And some arnica. Come on upstairs, you need a lie down. *(Helping him to his feet)* Yes, Magda'll be quite cosy in that spare room. Be a nice way to christen it, won't it? Are oboes very loud, do you know?

MARTIN. I've no idea.

HILDA. I mean, if she's practising at all hours … Well, we'll have to grin and bear it, I suppose …

(As they move off together, from outside the window, the distant sound of a fire engine.)

(looking out of the window) Oh, it's on the Mountjoy Estate, by the look of it. Something's blazing away down there, masses of smoke … *(Continuing on their way)* Come on, love, nothing for you to worry about. Upstairs now, gently now … gently …

(As they go off to the hall, music as the lights fade to:)

Scene Two

(The same. Later that day.)

(The music continues until **HILDA** *enters angrily.* **ROD** *follows anxiously close behind her.* **HILDA** *is digesting news she has just received from* **ROD**.*)*

HILDA. … and you're certain it was the Wrigleys?

ROD. Three big lads in ski masks kicking his front door in, threatening him, his wife and kids with baseball bats and knives, setting fire to the bloke's pigeon shed. Who else could it have been? Dudgeon recognised them, even with their masks on. They kept calling each other by name… The fire was most probably Duggie's doing. But all three, father and sons, Lee, Dirk and Duggie, they were all involved.

HILDA. There was no need to do that to pigeons. God's creatures.

ROD. I did say they were getting a bit out of hand.

HILDA. Out of hand? They've reduced us to the level of the people we were trying to … Where are they now? The Wrigleys?

ROD. Back home. Only a matter of time till the police catch up with them. Soon as they've sorted out their paperwork, they'll swoop. Well, this is a fine to-do, is this. Certainly put the cat among the—

HILDA. We instructed them to go round there and have a word with Dudgeon. A quiet word.

ROD. I think that was their idea of a quiet word. Has Martin been told yet?

HILDA. No. He's upstairs, resting after his – incident.

ROD. How is he?

HILDA. As well as can be expected. After being punched in the face by a madman.

ROD. Bradley's left, anyway. It's empty next door. Gone to stay in town, so I heard. Probably with his … woman …

HILDA. To stir up more trouble, no doubt.

(**ROD**'s *mobile rings.*)

ROD. *(consulting his screen)* Sorry, I'd better take this. It's the front gate. *(Answering)* Hallo ... Yes .... I see, alright. *(Muting the phone)* They say there's a police vehicle at the main gate demanding admission. Here to talk to the Wrigleys. What shall I tell them?

HILDA. Let them in, of course. They're the police. If necessary show them the way to the Wrigleys' house.

ROD. You sure?

HILDA. Of course. Full co-operation.

ROD. Only there's a chance they might feel a bit – aggrieved, you know.

HILDA. Who, the police?

ROD. No, the Wrigleys. The police'll be delighted. The Wrigleys might feel a bit, like – betrayed, you know.

HILDA. Betrayed? What do they expect us to do? Come out in support of arson? Violence? Destruction of wild life?

ROD. No, no. I wasn't saying that. But maybe they were expecting us to, you know, to provide them with an alibi. Say they were here with us, all the time.

HILDA. I'm certainly not lying for them. They've committed criminal acts, they must face the consequences. Now, let the police in, Rod. They're waiting for an answer.

ROD. *(uncertain)* Right. *(Into phone)* Hallo ... *(To* **HILDA***)* You're sure this'll be right with Martin?

HILDA. Of course it'll be right with him. Martin would never condone violence. *(As* **ROD** *makes to continue)* Wait! Is there anyone currently in the stocks?

ROD. Not currently. We released Ted Evans first thing this morning. On medical grounds. Suspected pneumonia.

HILDA. Right. Carry on. Might be awkward questions otherwise, if they saw that.

ROD. *(into phone)* Right. ... Let them in, Billy ... Yes, full co-operation. It's number eleven, remember. Right.

(He disconnects) All I'm saying, Hilda, is this might lead to repercussions.

HILDA. From the police?

ROD. No, the Wrigleys. They could maybe take it wrong. Especially Duggie.

HILDA. Well, that won't bother us. They'll all be locked up in jail, won't they?

ROD. *(doubtfully)* Possibly.

HILDA. I'd better go up and wake Martin. We have ten minutes before the meeting. I left him to sleep as long as he could. He needs all the rest he can get. Big day for him, tomorrow.

ROD. Oh, right. The press conference, eh? I hear they're all coming …

HILDA. Yes, they're here apparently. According to Dorothy. Television, the lot.

ROD. Television? Sooner him than me.

HILDA. Quite.

ROD. Standing up in front of them. All the cameras and so on. I wouldn't know where to start. But he's amazing, isn't he? Up there in front of people. Never lost for words, is he?

HILDA. He's a natural leader, Rod. Even as a little boy in the Boys' Brigade, in his little uniform. He led from the front even then.

ROD. A gift, isn't it?

HILDA. Born with it. Mind you, he works hard. It's not always as easy at it may look. He's been up all hours, working on this informal press statement for tomorrow.

ROD. Takes a sort of genius, doesn't it? I mean, begging his pardon, Hilda, I mean I'd never say this to Martin's face of course, but at first glance, you know, he's a bit like – almost unprepossessing – you know what I mean? *(digging himself deeper)* Dead ordinary, you know. Don't get me wrong, I wouldn't say it to his face, like. But insignificant, you know. Not someone you'd particularly notice. Average. You know what I mean – ? Ordinary.

(**HILDA**'s *silence speaks volumes.*)

Yes. I mean, he's a great bloke.

(*The doorbell rings.*)

HILDA. That'll be the others …

ROD. Listen, I think I'd best try and have a quick word with Lee Wrigley. Just to warn him the police are on their way. Try and make things straight. Straighter. Excuse me …

HILDA. *(shrugs)* Just as you like. It's up to you. I wouldn't bother.

(**HILDA** *goes out to the hall.*)

(**ROD** *speed dials his phone. As he speaks, he moves slowly to the kitchen door.*)

ROD. *(into phone)* Hallo, Lee … it's me, mate, Rod … Are they? Already? … Just the one car then? … No, I wouldn't advise that, Lee, I really wouldn't … No, well, I'm sorry you feel like that, I really do … no … no … I do understand … yes …

(**ROD** *goes off to the kitchen. As he does so, from the hall* **AMY** *enters, followed by an angry* **HILDA**.)

AMY. Thank you so much … *(She scans the empty room)*

HILDA. … how dare you come barging in here? You are not welcome in this house …

AMY. Not by you, obviously.

HILDA. Not by either of us. Martin certainly doesn't want to see you.

AMY. We'll ask him, shall we? Where is he?

HILDA. He has a meeting in five minutes. He doesn't want to see you.

AMY. How is he? I hear he got into a fight with Luther.

HILDA. Martin doesn't get into fights. It was unprovoked. Luther Bradley punched him in the face.

AMY. Oh, my God! Poor Martin. How is he?

HILDA. He's lying down, upstairs. Resting.

AMY. I'll go up to see him.

HILDA. *(outraged)* You're certainly not going into his bedroom.

AMY. Why not? *(Staring at **HILDA**)* God, you're unbelievable, Hilda, you really are. Talk about bearing grudges. You've never forgiven me, have you? I insulted your fucking awful wallpaper, your ghastly green paintwork …

HILDA. … this has nothing to do with wallpaper …

AMY. … your ghastly green paintwork – and you've never forgotten it, have you? It's unbelievable! I thought you called yourself a Christian, Hilda? Where did all that go, then? What happened to that?

HILDA. *(angrily)* You have brought my brother down to your own gutter level, haven't you? Creeping off together, every hour of the day …

AMY. *(amused)* Been following us then, have you …?

HILDA. … both of you, slithering off to that sleazy little hotel on the corner of West Street … that grubby pub in Straker Street with its unwashed curtains, sitting there with your glasses of whiskey …

AMY. My God! You really have been following us, haven't you? Hope you enjoyed yourself …

HILDA. Me? I wouldn't stoop that low. I wouldn't be seen dead in those places. I paid someone else to do it …

AMY. Who?

HILDA. Never mind. A professional. Someone who knows what she's doing.

AMY. It's Sindy, isn't it? Of course! My God, I saw her once. Or was it the other one, Cissy? You've really got those two on a leash, haven't you, Hilda? Little she-dogs. Well, what is it they say? Like attracts like …

HILDA. What do you mean by that?

*(Upstairs **MAGDA** starts practising her clarinet.)*

AMY. What on earth's that?

HILDA. It's Magda. She's staying with us. Practising in the guest bathroom.

AMY. Well. That should have woken him up. I'm going up to see him now. Which is his bedroom?

HILDA. *(stepping in front of* AMY*)* You are not going up there! I forbid it!

AMY. It's alright, I'll knock first. Make sure he's decent.

HILDA. Over my dead body, do you go up there.

AMY. OK, if necessary.

(They stand face to face, both refusing to yield.)

There's not going to be another punch up, surely?

HILDA. If need be. Though I warn you, my brother's the pacifist in this family. If you try and hit me, I'll hit you straight back.

(Before they can come to blows, the doorbell rings.)

AMY. Whoops. More guests. Look, this could all get a wee bit public, Hilda. Which is fine by me. How about you?

(Slight pause.)

HILDA. *(at length)* Top of the stairs. First door on the left.

AMY. Thank you. *(As she goes)* Don't worry, I'll re-make the bed afterwards.

(AMY goes out. HILDA is almost shaking with fury. She goes to the window and takes deep breaths in an effort to calm herself. Her lips are moving, as she prays for self control.)

(The doorbell rings again. MAGDA pauses in her practice, briefly.)

(ROD sticks his head in from the kitchen.)

ROD. That's the doorbell, Hilda. Are you going to go or you want me to?

HILDA. *(in a strangulated voice)* Yes … please … Would you go, Rod?

ROD. Right. You OK, Hilda?

HILDA. Yes. A little choking fit, that's all.

ROD. I'll let them in, then. Looks like Gareth and Dorothy …

HILDA. Ask them to wait in the kitchen, Rod. Martin will be down – in a minute.

(**ROD** *goes out to the front door.*)

(**HILDA** *stands for a moment longer. Then, coming to a sudden decision, she moves swiftly to the hall doorway.*)

(calling) Gareth! … Good evening, Dorothy … Gareth, I wonder if I could have a quiet word with you … just before the meeting …?

(**HILDA** *moves back into the room.* **GARETH** *enters clasping his files and folders for the forthcoming meeting.* **MAGDA** *resumes her playing*)

GARETH. *(as he enters)* Certainly. Good evening, Hilda … Sorry to hear about Martin's incident. Still, that man was always unstable … Bradley … even before … *(slightly tearful)* … you know … Amy's involvement …

HILDA. Yes, that's rather what I wanted to talk to you about, Gareth. Do sit down, won't you?

GARETH. Thank you. *(As* **MAGDA** *continues upstairs)* This is pleasant. Having a little musical accompaniment.

HILDA. Oh, yes.

GARETH. Atmospheric. Reminiscent of the royal palaces of mediaeval times. That'll be Magda, will it? Practising?

HILDA. Yes. I'll get her to stop before the meetings.

(*A slight pause.* **HILDA** *is deep in thought. During the next,* **MAGDA** *stops playing.*)

GARETH. Yes. Very pleasant. You fond of music, Hilda?

HILDA. Yes, in small doses.

GARETH. Clarinet, isn't it?

HILDA. I've no idea. Could be a ukulele as far as I'm concerned.

GARETH. *(laughing)* Yes, I'm fond of music. This type of music. Have it on all day. Classic FM. In my shed, whenever I'm tinkering. Yes. *(Rather nervously)* Was there something you wanted to discuss with me, Hilda?

HILDA. Yes. I've been giving a lot of thought recently to your own particular problem, Gareth ...

GARETH. Problem?

HILDA. As regards Amy. You know, she has treated you appallingly, Gareth ...

GARETH. She has.

HILDA. I've lain awake worrying about you ...

GARETH. She's not – you know, seeing Bradley – she's stopped that ...

HILDA. But has she stopped altogether, Gareth? Can you be sure?

GARETH. Probably not. Probably someone else by now entirely. She's still coming home at all hours with that stupid smile on her face, anyway. Reeking of whiskey. I don't know who it is, currently. No idea.

HILDA. As they say these days, don't let's even go there, Gareth.

GARETH. I'd sooner not.

HILDA. The fact remains, it's a scandal what that woman's been putting you through, Gareth. What your wife's been doing to you. And every time the subject comes up in committee, it's been glossed over, hasn't it?

GARETH. I feel it has, yes.

HILDA. What sort of example is she setting to the rest of Bluebell Hill? With her open drinking and her loose behaviour? Her appalling language, suggestive innuendos–? What sort of example is that for our young people? They see behaviour like that going unchecked, unpunished and they say to themselves, oh, if she can, the wife of a committee member, if she can behave like that, then why can't I ...? Before you know it, she's besmirched a whole generation, Gareth.

GARETH. Exactly.

HILDA. So I was wondering if you'd given any thought, you know – during your researches – into historic punishments, as to one which might fit the crime, if you see what I mean? Fitted this particular crime. Her crimes. Whether you'd come up with anything, during the course of your research?

GARETH. *(growing rather furtive)* Well, as a matter of fact, I have. I've given it a lot of thought, Hilda. I mean, lying alone there in the bed you know, especially … *(Opening his folder)* There's the obvious ones like – the stocks, of course – but they're not …

HILDA. No. Not really fitting, are they, in this case?

GARETH. *(turning a page)* Then there's this – our old friend the whipping post …

HILDA. *(less than enthusiastic)* Might turn her into a bit like a martyr then. People round here don't like seeing a woman whipped.

GARETH. *(another page)* And then there's this one. A scold's bridle? I've already made one of those … That ought to wipe the smile off her face. Fits round there … you see? With the spike.

HILDA. *(doubtful)* No …

GARETH. *(turning the page)* Chastity belt? That's quite fitting. I could run one of those up. *(Turning several more pages)* Various different designs, you see? That one's nasty …

HILDA. *(trying with difficulty not to avert her gaze)* Yes, that's all a bit private, isn't it? Rather too intimate. I was thinking of something more public.

GARETH. Ah, well now … *(Revealing another page)* How about this, then …?

HILDA. *(seeing something at last that interests her)* Oh, yes … that could be possible … very possible …

GARETH. I mean, the only problem is materials. They might prove a problem. Tar, for one. You can't lay your hand on tar that easily. Not unless there's road works in the locality. Which is rare with this council. But then I had a thought. I thought, paint. How about paint? Just as effective.

HILDA. Gloss or emulsion?

GARETH. Oh, gloss. Oil based. Needs to be oil based. Emulsion'd simply wash off. All we need is paint.

HILDA. We've got masses of paint here.

GARETH. There you go, then.

HILDA. In the hall cupboard out there. Left over. Almost a litre of the Pixie Green we used on these skirting boards. You're welcome to that …

GARETH. Perfect.

HILDA. Help yourself. I'll tell you what, Gareth, I'll ask the girls to give you a hand, shall I? Cissy and Sindy? They're a lovely pair, they're always willing to muck in.

GARETH. *(excited)* Right. Right.

*(**MAGDA** restarts practising.)*

HILDA. Gareth …

GARETH. What?

HILDA. This is our secret, remember. Just between us, no further. Keep it a surprise.

GARETH. Sure. This is officially sanctioned, is it? It doesn't need to pass through the D & P sub-committee.

HILDA. Well, after all the support the D & P have given you …

GARETH. It'll be OK with Martin? I'd hate to offend Martin.

HILDA. He'll be all for it. I'll run it past him, as soon as I get a moment. Oh, look at the time. Could you bring the others in from the kitchen while I fetch Martin?

*(**GARETH** moves to the kitchen doorway.)*

I must stop her making this dreadful noise too, it's driving me mad. See you in a minute.

GARETH. *(very excited)* OK, thank you, Hilda, thank you.

*(**HILDA** holds a finger to her lips.)*

(GARETH nods and goes to the kitchen doorway. HILDA goes off to the hall.)

GARETH. *(contd., calling)* You can come in, now ...

(DOROTHY returns with GARETH from the kitchen. Upstairs, shortly MAGDA stops her practising.)

DOROTHY. *(as they enter)* Rod's been on the phone for ages. Not good news, apparently.

GARETH. *(cheerfully)* Oh, dear.

DOROTHY. From the tone of his voice. I couldn't hear properly. Rod wouldn't let me listen. I tried ...

(MARTIN enters followed by HILDA. MARTIN appears to be in uncharacteristically good spirits. He smiles a lot.)

MARTIN. *(brightly and briskly)* Well, now, are we all met? Good evening, Dorothy! Good evening, Gareth!

GARETH. *(brightly)* Hallo, Martin.

DOROTHY. Hallo, Martin, dear. How are you feeling after your little rest? Has the lie down done you good?

MARTIN. Grand, Dorothy, thank you

HILDA. Seems to have done him the power of good.

DOROTHY. Nothing like a nice lie down in the daytime to relieve all your tensions. If you do it regularly, Martin, you'll really feel the benefit.

MARTIN. Right.

DOROTHY. No point in bottling it all up, is there?

HILDA. *(disapprovingly)* Yes, let's make a start, shall we? We're already very late, Chairman ...

MARTIN. Right, yes. Now. Oh, where's Rod?

GARETH. On the phone.

MARTIN. Oh, right. We'll hang on, then. You're looking a lot brighter this evening, Gareth.

GARETH. Oh, right. So are you.

MARTIN. Yes. Snap!

GARETH. Snap!

(ROD enters turning off his mobile.)

ROD. They've just been arrested.

MARTIN. Arrested? Who have?

ROD. The Wrigleys. Two of them, anyway. Typical police cock-up. Can you believe, they sent two officers. Two. One of them's barely an officer. It was a policewoman … That's all they sent … totally unarmed. Suicide mission. Heads should roll at that police station.

GARETH. They should.

DOROTHY. It's the hedge trimmer all over again, Rod. You know Rod was telling us, did he tell you about his –

MARTIN. Yes, but what happened at the Wrigleys?

ROD. Well, apparently the police weren't taking it too seriously, initially. Seeing as how the complaint came from Dudgeon who's almost as bent as the Wrigleys. As they saw it, one villain complaining about another. Standard gang rivalry …

MARTIN. Well, I think we've certainly been misled as to the reputation of the Wrigleys, Rod. I had no idea they were known criminals.

HILDA. We certainly didn't.

ROD. Well, the way I saw it, I thought when the Wrigleys weren't working for us, what they got up to in their spare time, was best left unsaid. I thought you should know – only what you needed to.

HILDA. We certainly needed to know if they were involved in criminal activities. We never intended to run our neighbourhood watch scheme on fear, did we?

ROD. Well, not exactly fear. Just the occasional warning. The occasional friendly warning, you know …

HILDA. Like the warning they gave to Mr Dudgeon?

MARTIN. What warning was that?

ROD. They set fire to his pigeons.

MARTIN. Oh, dear heaven …

HILDA. I still see those poor little birds, you know. Fluttering and blazing …

DOROTHY. Terrible. No need for that.

(From the hall, the front door opens and slams.)

ROD. What was that?

GARETH. Front door.

HILDA. Possibly Magda.

MARTIN. Yes, possibly. Going out for a breath of air.

(From upstairs MAGDA *plays a brief snatch of clarinet.)*

(unconvincingly) Oh, no. It can't have been. Oh, I remember now. I – did open the front door – just now – to see – to see if was raining – didn't I, Hilda?

HILDA. Yes.

MARTIN. And I must have left it – open. Silly me.

ROD. Was it?

MARTIN. What?

ROD. Raining?

MARTIN. Yes. No. I didn't really notice.

ROD. *(as unconvinced by this as everyone)* Yes. Anyway, to continue. Unsurprisingly, the Wrigleys resisted arrest and there followed an almighty dust up which also involved Maeve, Mrs Wrigley, as well –

DOROTHY. The mother?

ROD. Who is not to be trifled with, either. Resulting in some minor collateral damage to the policewoman and the male copper sustaining a suspected multiple fracture. Two of the Wrigleys, father and son, were handcuffed and put in the car, the third one got clean away and is now on the loose, roaming Bluebell Hill.

GARETH. Duggie?

ROD. Duggie. Out there somewhere. Baying for vengeance.

HILDA. Vengeance?

ROD. On us.

DOROTHY. Us?

ROD. This committee.

HILDA. Do you think I should lock the window?

MARTIN. Sensible precaution, Hilda.

(**HILDA** *goes to the window.*)

MARTIN. (*contd.*) Now. I don't think there's any cause for undue alarm. The police are dealing with this …

ROD. Giving us every cause for alarm …

MARTIN. Now, now, Rod, we know your opinion of the police and that is duly noted but with respect there is a vast difference between retrieving a hedge trimmer which may or may not have been stolen …

ROD. It was stolen! Red handed the bugger …!

MARTIN. … and the capture and apprehension of a violent criminal who may or may not be armed …

ROD. He's almost certainly armed –

MARTIN. … but we can be assured, the police will no doubt be formulating a response to this, even as we speak …

ROD. You bet they will be. Injuring two of their own? Hell hath no fury like a policeman maimed … They'll be all over us. This time, they won't just send a single squad car. There'll be armoured troop carriers, SWAT teams, trained marksmen, riot gear, the lot.

DOROTHY. Oh, dear.

ROD. Tasers, tear gas … in half an hour's time, mark my words, there'll be a ring of steel around this whole development. No one'll be safe. Armageddon.

HILDA. (*still at the window*) Well, at least Jesus is still out here. Looking out for us.

ROD. With respect to your religious beliefs, Hilda, I think it'll take a damn sight more than a twelve inch plaster statue of our Saviour to stop Duggie Wrigley, let alone a fully armoured SWAT team.

HILDA. Martin? What are we going to do?

(*They all look at him.*)

DOROTHY. Yes. What's our chairman say?

MARTIN. (*after a pause, deliberately*) I think we should probably adjourn the meeting at this stage, ladies and gentlemen, and return immediately to our respective homes and continue life, as far as possible, in a normal manner. Clearly the immediate danger, till he's caught, is Duggie who appears to have developed a personal vendetta against this committee. Whom he feels for some reason has betrayed him. And in particular, as chairman, very probably against my individual self.

(Silence.)

Any comments? Anybody anything to add? Any other business, then?

(No response.)

(Rising) Right. Meeting closed. Thank you, everyone. Sleep well. Hopefully see you all tomorrow. I presume the press conference is still going ahead, Dorothy?

DOROTHY. So far as I know. They'll be even more interested if they think there's going to be a gun battle.

MARTIN. *(smiling)* I trust it won't come to that. *(Moving to the door)* I'll see you all out.

*(**MARTIN** goes into the hall. **ROD** and **DOROTHY** follow him. **GARETH** follows them.)*

ROD. *(as he goes)* 'night!

DOROTHY. Goodnight, Hilda. Take care, won't you?

HILDA. Goodnight, Rod. 'night, Dorothy

*(**ROD** and **DOROTHY** go out to the hall.)*

(softly) Gareth. Don't forget your paint, will you? It's in the cupboard there, under the stairs. The green.

GARETH. We're still going ahead with that, then?

HILDA. You heard what Martin said. Life to continue in a normal manner.

GARETH. Right.

*(**HILDA** picks up a scatter cushion from the sofa.)*

HILDA. And, Gareth. You'll be needing this.

*(**HILDA** tosses him the cushion, which he catches.)*

GARETH. *(puzzled)* What?

HILDA. That's full of duck feathers. Don't worry, I won't be wanting it back.

*(***GARETH*** *stares at the cushion, then at* **HILDA** *and then hurries out, guiltily hiding the cushion behind his back as he does so.)*

(The front door closes a second or so later and in a moment, **MARTIN** *returns.)*

MARTIN. Well, now. All we can do is wait, can't we? I hope he doesn't get in. I don't think I'll be so lucky with Duggie Wrigley if I get away with a simple punch in the face.

HILDA. This is all my fault, I'm sorry

MARTIN. Your fault? Why should it be your fault, Hilda?

HILDA. I told them to let the police in.

MARTIN. No, you did the correct thing, Hilda.

HILDA. Rod was right, we should have all stuck together and given the Wrigleys an alibi. Say they were here with us all the time. Then the police would have had to leave them alone ...

MARTIN. Hilda, that would have been lying. A flat lie. We can't condone lying. Not to the police. Just to protect criminal – thugs. I mean, it's a slippery slope, Hilda, once you start ... Once you start lying it's impossible ever to stop. You get into the habit. The habit of deceit. You heard us both just now. When that front door slammed. Pretending we didn't know it was Amy. "I was just looking out to see if it was raining." It was pathetic. *(Smiling)* I almost blushed with embarrassment.

HILDA. You did. *(She looks at him tenderly)* Oh, Martin.

MARTIN. What?

HILDA. *(hugging him)* You're such a good man. Such a good, good, good man.

MARTIN. *(modestly)* Well. So says you.

HILDA. So says everybody. They all do. You must get some rest. Big day tomorrow.

MARTIN. Oh, yes. I think I'll sleep down here tonight, you know, Hilda. Keep an eye out. Just in case he tries to get in.

HILDA. What are you going to do against him? Against Duggie?

MARTIN. At least I can give you and Magda an early warning.

(A pause.)

Hilda, I need to say something to you. I really do.

HILDA. Can't it wait till morning?

MARTIN. No. I think you know what I'm going to say.

HILDA. Yes, I think I know what you're going to say, Martin, I just don't want to hear you saying it. Not tonight.

MARTIN. It'll be the same in the morning. I need to move away, Hilda.

HILDA. Move away?

MARTIN. From here. Not immediately. Certainly I'll go through with the press conference tomorrow. Even stay on with the committee for a bit, as chairman. If you'll all have me.

HILDA. It's her, isn't it?

MARTIN. No. Not altogether …

HILDA. Her.

MARTIN. No, Hilda, you mustn't blame her entirely. Amy may have been the trigger but I was restless even before … I think, in my mind, I was looking for a way out. You know, a fresh start. Amy's just provided the doorway, that's all …

HILDA. *(irritated)* What doorway? What are you talking about, doorway?

MARTIN. Doorway to – freedom.

HILDA. *(smiling wryly)* Freedom …!

MARTIN. I'm trapped, Hilda. Both of us are. I mean look at us, you and me, brother and sister. Still living together. Getting on for fifty, aren't we?

HILDA. You know what Father said about freedom. Unfettered freedom is the devil's delusion …

MARTIN. Well, Father had some very queer ideas, didn't he? I can see that now. I mean, let's face it, we're both going to be standing here, exactly the same when we're seventy, aren't we? And we'll still have done nothing …

HILDA. We'll have done everything! Everything God intended us to do … We'll have lived good lives. Proper, decent lives, Martin.

MARTIN. I don't think this is what He was intending me to do. I hope not. Organising neighbourhood watch schemes that go off at half cock. End up like – like this. Terrified to go out because there's an unhappy misguided maniac out there who wants to try and kill us. SWAT teams. I mean, we've made it worse. I can deal with little lads with clarinet cases, I'm not sure I can cope with fully grown ones with baseball bats.

(A pause.)

HILDA. We're experiencing a temporary setback, that's all.

MARTIN. Listen, I know that you and Amy … you're hardly on the best of terms at present. But I think you can really grow to respect each other, in time. You're both – well, in my eyes anyway, you're both wonderful people. Different, you know, but … Anyway, I wanted you to know there'll always be a place for you in my home, our home, Amy's and mine, wherever we are, there'll always be room for you, Hilda.

*(A silence. **HILDA** is frozen-faced.)*

I probably haven't put that as well as I might have done, but ….

HILDA. She's a whore, Martin.

MARTIN. Sorry?

HILDA. She's a prostitute. No better than that …

MARTIN. I'm sorry you feel like that.

HILDA. How could you consider living – co-habiting with a woman like that? You? You, of all people? A truly good man grovelling in the dirt … for that worthless …

*(**HILDA** moves to the hall doorway. When she turns, we see she is crying.)*

MARTIN. *(trying to lighten it)* Well, there are noble precedents for that, you know, Hilda. For good men to consort with prostitutes. Surely?

HILDA. Yes, maybe there are. But He only used them to wash His feet, didn't He?

(She goes out to the hall. Soon, somewhere distant, we hear her bedroom door slam.)

MARTIN. *(shaking his head sadly, to himself)* Oh, Hilda. Hilda, Hilda, Hilda, Hilda. What am I going to do with you, girl?

(He moves to the window.)

All quiet on the western front.

(He goes to the hall doorway and switches off the lights. The room is now illuminated only by the security light outside the window.)

*(**MARTIN** moves to the sofa, lies down and tries to make himself comfy.)*

(wriggling) Maybe this wasn't such a good idea of mine.

(He finds one of the pair of scatter cushions.)

Where's the other one of these cushions gone? Can't have been nicked, surely? Dear, oh dear. I don't know … I don't know … I don't know …

(He lies on the sofa with just the light from the window. He falls asleep almost immediately.)

(The outside security light goes out sharply. Darkness.)

(It is unclear just how much time has passed, when the quality of light from the window changes hue till the room is lit from the light of silent flames, gentle at first,

*then growing more fierce, gradually illuminating the
room with eerie dancing shadows.)*

(The sound of an approaching fire engine. Then another.
MARTIN *slumbers on.)*

(HILDA *enters hurriedly from the hall. She is fully
dressed.)*

HILDA. *(quietly and urgently)* Martin! Martin! Wake up!

(HILDA *pauses in the doorway.)*

(vainly trying the light switch) Oh, no! There's no lights
in here, either. What's happened to all the lights?

*(She goes to the sofa, groping with difficulty in the
darkness, and shakes* **MARTIN** *awake.)*

Martin! Martin! Wake up!

MARTIN. *(waking)* Wha –? Now listen, Duggie, old lad, we
can talk about this –

HILDA. Martin, it's me! Next door's on fire …

MARTIN. Next doo –? The house –? You mean –? Oh, no!

(MARTIN *moves to the window, craning to get a better
view of the fire.)*

(Simultaneously, **MAGDA** *hurries on from the hall. She is
still in her night things)*

MAGDA. *(in a panic)* Next door's on fire! My house is on
fire. I saw it from the window –

HILDA. Yes, we know it is, Magda, dear …

MARTIN. It's well alight. It's blazing away …

MAGDA. What are we going to do? What are we going to
do?

MARTIN. They seem to be tackling it. They must have
brought the fire engines in from the front. No sign of
anyone out the back here, anyway.

HILDA. *(moving to the window)* Will it spread to us? Does it
look as if it's going to spread?

MARTIN. It might. If they don't get it under control soon.

MAGDA. What are we going to do? What are we going to do?

HILDA. Oh, do be quiet, Magda, Martin's trying to think …

MARTIN. *(decisively)* Right. Best be on the safe side. Both of you, go upstairs now, gather up – er – your vital bits and pieces, the things you can carry, and we'll all meet up out there in the hall in two minutes. Alright?

HILDA. Right.

MARTIN. Magda?

MAGDA. Yes?

MARTIN. Have you got that?

MAGDA. Yes.

MARTIN. Then go, girl. Go, go, go!

(MAGDA runs out.)

HILDA. *(calling after her)* And put some clothes on!

(MARTIN moves to follow her.)

(To MARTIN) Where are you going?

MARTIN. Going to check front and rear, make sure Duggie's not out there lying in wait for us. All the security lights are out. This may be his plan. Wait there in the dark. Try to smoke us out. Now go upstairs, Hilda. Do as you're told for once, woman.

(MARTIN goes off swiftly to the hall.)

(HILDA lingers and moves to the window.)

HILDA. *(cupping her hands to the glass)* I think … I think they've cut away our fence. It seems to have gone. *(Seeing something)* Oh, no, he's still out there … We can't … we can't … Martin …

(MARTIN returns.)

MARTIN. What are you doing, Hilda? I told you to go upstairs.

HILDA. We can't leave him out there. We can't leave him.

MARTIN. Who?

HILDA. Jesus. He's still out there.

MARTIN. Oh, leave him. He'll be fine …

HILDA. But he might get burnt. He can't be burnt …

MARTIN. *(impatiently)* Oh, for goodness sake, here …

> *(**MARTIN** pushes past **HILDA** and goes off into the garden.)*

HILDA. Oh, Martin, thank you … Thank you … *(Watching him)* Carefully …

> *(**MARTIN** returns with the small plaster statue of Jesus in peaceful pose, as if blessing those around him.)*

> *(As **MARTIN** steps back through the windows, a bright searchlight from the garden catches him in its beam.)*

> *(**MARTIN** freezes. **HILDA** instinctively steps back out of the bright light, shielding her eyes. A voice from a police loud hailer is heard from the garden.)*

VOICE. *(from the garden)* This is the police. You are ordered to throw down your weapon and step outside with your hands raised …

MARTIN. Oh, heavens!

HILDA. It's the police.

MARTIN. I know it is, Hilda. I can hear.

HILDA. What are you going to do?

MARTIN. Better do as they say …

VOICE. *(from the garden)* This is an official police warning. You are ordered to throw down your weapon and to step outside with your hands raised …

MARTIN. They think I've got a weapon …

HILDA. Tell them you haven't got one …

MARTIN. *(shouting)* I haven't got a weapon. See? This is not a weapon. It's Jesus … *(He holds up the figure for them to see)*

VOICE. *(from the garden)* This is your final warning. Throw your weapon on the ground now and proceed outside with your hands in the air.

MARTIN. *(shouting)* I said, it isn't a weapon. I can't throw this on the ground, it'll break! It's Jesus. Look! See!

*(**MARTIN** steps through the window and into the garden, brandishing the figure as he goes.)*

(calling as he goes) See here! Look, can you see? It's Jesus …!

*(**MARTIN** disappears out of sight.)*

See? It's Jesus! Je-

(A single rifle shot from the garden cuts off his final word.)

HILDA. *(a scream)* Martin!

MARTIN. *(his painful dying words)* Oh … Jesus …

(Music.)

*(During this **HILDA** steps out into the garden, her arms raised.)*

(As she goes the lights cross fade to:)

Scene Three

(The same.)

(A few days later.)

*(**AMY** is shown in by **MAGDA**.)*

(Judging from their dress, it is evidently the day of the funeral.)

*(**MAGDA**, in particular, is in sombre clothes.)*

*(**AMY**, characteristically, has included a dash of colour.)*

AMY. Thanks.

MAGDA. She'll be down in a minute. She's – she's just getting – ready.

AMY. Yes. Thanks.

*(**AMY** moves to the window, **MAGDA** straightens the room and then remains by the door. There is awkwardness between them.)*

Oh, you've got your view back.

*(**MAGDA** does not reply.)*

Much nicer without the fence. Bit like a prison camp, wasn't it?

*(**MAGDA** does not reply.)*

(craning round to see next door) Oh, dear. What a mess. Sad. Your poor old house. Not much of it left, is there? Still, I suppose you can count yourself lucky Duggie targeted the wrong house. If he'd set fire to this one, all three of you'd have been … Yep.

*(**MAGDA** is silent. In a moment, **HILDA** enters dressed in black. **AMY** turns.)*

HILDA. Good morning.

AMY. Hilda, thanks for seeing me, I –

HILDA. Thank you, Magda. Perhaps you'd wait by the front door, dear? Look out for our car?

(**MAGDA** *goes out.*)

AMY. *(awkwardly, for her)* I'm not really sure why I'm here really. Except I wanted a word with you, personally, before it all got hopelessly busy with the funeral ... everyone ... all the press and ... so on. I wanted to say – I really feel so sad. For you. And for me. I think we both loved him very much, didn't we?

HILDA. I certainly loved him.

AMY. Well, I think I did, too. In my way. In a different way. In my case, rather more now than I knew I loved him when he was alive. He – I realise now – he was very special.

HILDA. He was. He was a very special man.

AMY. Yes. I mean, I know you don't think much of me. We never did get on, did we? Maybe because of our love for Martin. It may have got in the way. Still, if it's any consolation for you today, any – comfort. It's just to let you know that with him gone – someone else's heart has been broken, too.

(**HILDA** *inclines her head in acknowledgment.*)

(**AMY** *seems relieved to have said that.*)

(more brightly) Yes. That's all I came to say. I probably said it all upside down and in the wrong order. But that's me. I'm always hopeless whenever I try to get remotely serious. I always come out and say all the – *(At the window, again)* Oh, dear, oh, look. You've lost your little man, haven't you? I mean, sorry, Jesus. You've lost Jesus, haven't you? You must miss him. I suppose they must have taken him as evidence. Ironic, isn't it? Mistaking Jesus for a lethal weapon. *(She laughs nervously)*

(Silence.)

Yes. Well, I must be ... I'll probably see you at the church. Amidst the throng. But in case I don't ... *(At the hall doorway)* You know this room tends to grow on you ... I have to admit I'm almost coming round to

your green paint. *(She laughs)* Not quite. But nearly. See
you.

HILDA. Goodbye. I'd give you a lift to the church only …

AMY. No, that's OK. I'm already getting a lift from the girls,
Cissy and Sindy. They're coming round to pick us both
up. Gareth and me. They offered, right out of the
blue, wasn't that sweet of them? 'bye.

*(**AMY** goes out. The front door closes.)*

HILDA. *(calling)* Magda! Magda!

*(**MAGDA** comes from the hall.)*

MAGDA. It's just pulling up outside. Lovely big car.

HILDA. Yes, well, it's a special occasion, Magda, isn't it?
Now, when we get home afterwards, what do we need
to remember not to do today?

MAGDA. Not to practise.

HILDA. Good girl. Just for today. No clarinets or oboes or
cor français – or whatever you call them …

MAGDA. *(giggling)* Cor anglais.

HILDA. *(smiling)* Anglais, then.

MAGDA. *(giggling)* Cor français!

*(She impulsively kisses **HILDA** on the mouth.)*

Oh, I love you so much. I really love you.

HILDA. *(gently admonishing her)* Now, we mustn't do that
when we're outside, Magda. Only in the house, dear.
It's alright when we're on our own indoors, but never
out there.

MAGDA. *(chastened)* No.

HILDA. Otherwise what are people going to think? *(Taking
MAGDA's hand)* Come along, then … We don't want to
be late.

MAGDA. *(as they leave, sulkily)* Why's that woman coming?
That Amy? She's so – Why is she going to Martin's
funeral? She shouldn't be there, should she?

HILDA. She's not, my darling, she won't be there, don't worry ...

*(**HILDA** and **MAGDA** make to leave.)*

*(**MAGDA** goes off. As she does so, the band strikes up as at the start.)*

*(**HILDA** steps into her original position in the solo spot she was in at the top of the play. The area of light widens again and, as if it has just been unveiled, we get our first view of the Martin Massie memorial statue, a human sized bronze of Montmorency, the garden gnome, affectionately known as Monty.)*

*(As the band finishes playing, over its dying notes, a recording of **MARTIN**'s voice is heard over the PA sound system.)*

MARTIN. *(his recorded voice)* ... there is someone here for you! Speaking out for you! Fighting your corner! And that man is here, standing in front of you today!

(An enthusiastic burst of applause is heard on the recording.)

(Recorded voice, over the applause) Thank you and bless you all!

(The recording cuts off abruptly as the lights fade rapidly to:-)

(A blackout.)

End of play.